D0097161

More Than Conquerors

by
Terry Mize

...In all these things we are more than conquerors
through him that loved us.
Romans 8:37

Terry Mize Ministries
P.O. Box 35044
Tulsa, OK 74153

Unless otherwise indicated, all Scripture quotations are taken from the *King James Version* of the Bible.

More Than Conquerors
ISBN 978-0-9723568-0-0

Copyright © 1979, 1981, 1990 by Terry Mize
P.O. Box 35044
Tulsa, OK 74153

Published by **Terry Mize Ministries**
P.O. Box 35044
Tulsa, OK 74153

Contents

Foreword

Very few men or women on the mission field today are living up to the calling that God has put on their lives. Actually, the word *missionary* does not appear in the New Testament. The more I study God's Word, the more I am convinced that people with the missionary calling on their lives actually are apostles and should be walking in apostolic power.

I know you will be as excited as I was when I first read this book by Terry Mize. It is exciting to see a man walk in the apostolic power and calling God has put upon his life.

I have watched Terry Mize grow in faith over the years. I have watched his boldness. I have watched his ministry produce for the Kingdom of God. I am thrilled and honored to have a part in this book and in the ministry of this man of faith.

There is no thrill like the thrill of walking in the anointing of God. To experience that anointing is to experience life at its highest and best on this earth. To see people's needs met right before your very eyes; to see God move in His power and glory; to watch the Son of God, Jesus of Nazareth, glorified before men is the most fabulous adventure God ever planned for men.

The outstanding thing we are learning in this day and hour is that an anointing of power is available not only to men and women on the mission field, or men and women in the pulpit, but to any member of the Body of Christ who will make himself or herself available for Jesus to use.

Read this book. Get all excited. Then read it again. Read it again and again, until you realize that it is about

God's Word, not just the special calling or special ministry that God has placed on Terry and Jackie Mize.

The Word is where the power is. God's Word is His power.

We are living in the days prophesied of old. We are living in the days the prophets of old desired to see and take part in. Let's all be determined to take our places in this great endtime move of the Spirit of God. Jesus is coming so soon — even sooner than any of us can think or comprehend.

As you read this book, make the decision to take your place and do your part. Together with the Word of God, the power of the Holy Spirit, the full armor of God, prayer, the name of Jesus, and all the great things of the Body of Christ working together for us, we can do anything God calls upon us to do. We can do anything that is necessary to bring the nations to the knowledge that Jesus Christ of Nazareth is alive and well. Together, we can do it!

May the Lord bless you, and may His very best continue to manifest in your life is my prayer for you.

Jesus is Lord!

Kenneth Copeland
Fort Worth, Texas

C H A P T E R 1

Hitchhiker!
• • •

Let me begin this book with an event that happened to me. You may have heard it, because other ministers tell it also: some have even included it in their books.

I share it with you not just because it's an exciting missionary war story, but because it demonstrates the integrity of God's Word, the power of the name of Jesus, and the authority of the believer.

These same principles will work for anyone who uses them. They are God's Word, and His Word works.

In October of 1974, my wife, Jackie, and I lived in Guadalajara, Mexico, working as missionaries. A friend of ours, Randy Nichols, bought an organ and public address system for our work in Mexico. I had to drive to Houston, Texas, to pick it up and bring it back to Mexico. We had just been given a new car a few months before. (This was one of many cars the Lord has given us. I love God's payment plan — nothing down and no monthly payments.)

DISCOURAGING WORDS CAN KILL YOU
• • •

Just prior to leaving Mexico, I was talking to another missionary who said, "Terry, you know we missionaries

7

have to be prepared at any time to suffer for Jesus. Sometimes we go out in villages and get leeches, lice, ticks, fleas, bedbugs — all kinds of things. We have to go through all kinds of hardships — drinking bad water, and eating bad food and getting sick from it."

He continued, "We just have to put up with these things. It's our reasonable service. We might even be preaching in some remote village and some drunk could shoot us and kill us. That's the missionary's lot in life."

At this point, I said, "Are you finished?"

"I guess so," he replied. "Why?"

"My brother," I stated, "I don't know what page of the missionary handbook you got that stuff from, but you did not get it out of the Word of God."

I understood his concern, because I had been and had lived in those places. You cannot imagine some of the conditions missionaries encounter — bad water, food and so forth. It takes a special anointing to eat monkey liver, fish eyeballs, rat soup and other delicacies around the world. I've done it. I know!

I continued, "I've not participated in this 'get sick and get bugs program.' I've prayed and believed God and His Word. When I went on my first missionary trip at age eighteen with the Choco Indians in the jungles of Panama, I learned quickly to believe God to not get leeches and other bugs. The Indians would sometimes have to scrape a missionary's body with hunting knives to get the leeches off, but I never got one."

I said, "As far as the food goes, the Word of God says that I can drink any deadly thing, and it will not hurt me." (Mark 16:18.)

I am so glad the Holy Spirit put that in the Bible! There are some scriptures I believe He included just for missionaries. One of them is, "Eat what is set before you." (1 Corinthians 10:27.) That is one missionary scripture I wish was not in the Word! But I do not even ask what I am eating anymore. I just say, "Thank You, Lord," and eat it!

I told the man with the discouraging words that I had learned how to believe God.

I said, "All of us have the Word of God. We do not have to put up with bugs or get sick. If some guy comes up and shoots me, who have I helped?

"If I leave my wife and family in Guadalajara to drive way up in the villages — up into the mountains where nobody has any idea who I am — and some drunk comes along and shoots me because I am preaching the Word of God, or because he does not like the way I look, or because he is full of the devil, who have I helped?

"My family would never see me again. They would not know what had happened to me. I have not helped them, and I have not helped the villagers to whom I am preaching. They would decide what I was preaching was not true, because it did not really work.

"And I have not helped the guy who shoots me. I have just added murder to his problems. That is a cop-out. All I would be doing is taking a one-way trip to heaven.

"I will tell you what! If some guy pulls a gun on me, I will pull the Word of God on him and win him over with it!"

MY FAITH GETS TESTED
· · ·

Soon afterwards, I went to Houston to pick up the organ and the public address system. Just getting that equipment into Mexico is another testimony! It is illegal to even bring an electric can opener into Mexico, much less all the stuff I was bringing back.

When I reached the Texas-Mexico border, I had to list each piece of equipment with the border guards and almost threaten to call down fire from heaven on them to get to keep it!

When I finally did get admitted into Mexico, I spent the night in a little town called Zacatecas.

The next morning, I took off for Guadalajara, about four or five hours away. I had been gone about ten days and was anxious to get back home. Jackie had given birth to our second little boy, and I had taken them home from the hospital just before I left for Houston.

As I pulled out of Zacatecas, I saw a hitchhiker standing by the side of the road. At first, I passed him by, but then I was really impressed that the man needed Jesus. Now, God did not speak to me and tell me to pick him up. But I stopped the car and backed up; he got in, and we started off down the road.

After gathering my Spanish together to tell him about Jesus, I turned to say something to him — and there he sat with a gun in his hand!

When he saw me look at the gun, he shoved it into my ribs, reached up with his left hand, grabbed my collar, and started screaming and yelling at me, "I am going to kill you!"

I said, "You cannot do that, I am a man of God."

Again he screamed and yelled at me that he was going to kill me, and again I said, "You cannot do that. I am a man of God."

When I saw the gun in his hand, the first thing that happened, of course, was that my heart jumped up in my throat. The unexpected sight of the gun scared me! But I knew enough about the Word of God to know that fear and faith are opposites.

FEAR IS THE OPPOSITE OF FAITH
. . .

Satan is motivated by fear. God is motivated by faith. Faith and fear cannot operate in the same place. I knew that, so I got rid of fear by simply saying to myself:

"**For God hath not given us the spirit of fear; but of power, and of love, and of a sound mind** (2 Timothy 1:7); **fear hath torment, but perfect love casteth out fear** (1 John 4:18); **God is love** (1 John 4:16b), and I have God. So, fear, get out of here in the name of Jesus! I am not tolerating you!"

After I had dispatched fear, I had to deal with another situation: mental assent. I believe it was Frances Hunter who called people "goat Christians."

They say, "I believe the Word of God, *but....*" They are always "butting" everything: "Sure, I believe the Word of God says we are healed by the stripes of Jesus, *but* I have this pain. I know God is my source, *but* my bank book is empty."

That is "mentally assenting" to the Word of God. That is not true belief and certainly not faith. "Goat Christians" believe the Word but act in agreement with the circumstances.

At that moment of crisis in Mexico, I had to "know that I know that I know" I believed the Word of God.

I had been listening to a message on my tape player by Kenneth Copeland entitled, "The Integrity of the Word of God." So I just let the tape keep running. If there was ever a time I needed to hear that message, it was then!

As I drove along, the hitchhiker kept screaming that he was going to kill me, and I kept saying, "You cannot do that. I am a man of God. I have authority over you, in the name of Jesus. You cannot kill me; you cannot harm me in any way."

He could not understand that. According to the world's "rational" thinking, it did not look as though I had authority over the situation at all.

If you had been sitting beside the road in a bleacher watching all of that taking place, who would you have thought was winning?

Most people would say, "The guy with the gun."

However, the Bible says, "The man with the Word of God wins!"

I rebuked that hitchhiker in English, in Spanish, and in tongues. I reminded God what His Word said. I told both the devil and the man what the Word of God had to say. At the same time, I was hearing it all and reminding myself of the Word. **Faith cometh by hearing, and hearing by the word of God** (Romans 10:17).

FAITH MUST OPERATE THROUGH A RENEWED MIND
• • •

However, my mind was going a million miles a minute. You know how your mind operates when there is an emergency. The devil brought back to me all the tricks I had seen on television. I thought about slamming on the brakes and grabbing the gun — I thought about all of those possibilities!

Once my friend, Jerry Savelle, was telling the story of what happened to me, and he said:

"If Terry's mind had been renewed to television detectives, he would have done what they do. But since his mind was renewed to the Word of God, he used the Word of God."

You have to keep your Word-level higher than any other level. I was glad I knew that the Word of God was life to me, because I was in a situation where I had an opportunity to *not* live very long.

I told the hitchhiker I was a minister. He did not know what a minister was.

I told him I was a preacher. He knew nothing about a preacher.

I told him I was like a priest, and since Mexico was mostly Catholic, he knew what a priest was. But he was not in real good standing with his local church, so he was not very impressed that I was a priest.

He just kept telling me he was going to kill me, and I kept telling him that he was not.

I said to God, "Now, Father, Jesus said I have authority or power over all authority of the enemy. All! And nothing — nothing — shall by any means hurt me." (Luke 10:19.)

I was releasing my faith with words, which I was glad about later on.

I said, "God, if he pulls the trigger, my job is to believe Your Word, and Your job is to do something about that bullet. Your job is to do something with that bullet, and You do not have much room to work with because the barrel is against my side."

That may sound funny now, but it was not funny then. I said that to God because I believed it, and I still believe it today.

Some places where I share this testimony, a person will come up to me and say, "I have a testimony just like that — except I got robbed."

YOUR WORDS MAKE THE DIFFERENCE
· · ·

I have to tell those people their testimony is *not* really like mine. I did not lose; I won.

If I take the time to listen to them, I will find out where they missed it. One man told me that he had a testimony just like mine — except he got shot.

He said, "I picked up a hitchhiker who pulled a gun on me, and I said, 'Hallelujah!' and he shot me."

I said, "Well, that was because of what you said."

The difference is in what you say.

A woman wrote me from South Mexico, "Terry, I wish you had been here with your faith and deliverance ministry, but you probably could not have handled this guy either. He was demon-possessed. We had him locked up, but he broke loose and came after my husband. My husband said, 'The blood of Jesus has power,' but the guy hit him anyway."

I wrote back that her husband might just as well have said, "The grass is green, and the sky is blue."

14

All he did was make a statement of truth. He stated a fact with no action accompanying his words. Sure, the blood of Jesus has power, but he could have said, "The sun is going to rise tomorrow," and made a statement of truth. Stating facts or truths is not effective in itself.

The man should have said, "Satan, stop right there! You will not touch God's anointed! Do not take another step! Now, devil, get out of him in the name of Jesus!"

I kept saying this to the hitchhiker, and he kept getting madder and madder at me. Each time the devil would bring thoughts to my mind, I would just reach up and catch myself by the ear with my left hand and say, "Now Terry, you say what the Word of God says. You handle this in the Spirit."

You know, Elijah simply said, "Let us let God be God. If Baal is god, then we will serve him. If God is God, we will serve Him." (1 Kings 18:21.)

God showed Himself strong, and Elijah killed all the prophets of Baal. (1 Kings 18:24,40.)

I said, "God, I am going to let You be God. I am going to handle this in the Spirit. I refuse to do anything in the flesh. I am going to use the Word of God on this guy, and I am going to have to win. I am more than a conqueror!"

The more I talked, the madder he got. What I was saying did not make any sense to him. He had the gun in my ribs, the hammer cocked, and his finger on the trigger, but I was not acting according to his expectations.

Once, he asked me, "Aren't you afraid?"

I said, "Why should I be afraid? All you have is a loaded gun, but I have the name of Jesus."

He reached down and picked up one of the microphones lying on the seat beside me, and I said, "Put that down! It belongs to God. Everything in this car belongs to God. I belong to God, the car belongs to God, and you cannot have any of it!"

That just made him madder, and he said, "Pull over in this cornfield, off on the side of the road. Pull in there!

When I pulled into the cornfield, he reached over, grabbed the keys out of the ignition, and yelled. "Get out!"

I got out of the car on my side, and he got out on his side. Then he ordered me to go to the front of the car and said, "Give me your money, your watch, your rings, and your sunglasses. Lay them on the ground there, then back up."

I did as I was told. Then he walked up and bent down to pick up everything.

When he got close to me, I stuck my finger in his face and said, "I rebuke you in the name of Jesus Christ of Nazareth!"

He stuck the gun between my eyes — hammer still cocked and finger on the trigger — and was wildly slinging his left hand.

"Shut up!" he yelled. "If you say one more word, I will kill you!"

I stuck my finger back in his face, past his gun, and said, "I rebuke you in the name of Jesus Christ of Nazareth, and you cannot kill me or hurt me in any way!"

Instantly, he jumped back, lowered his gun, and shot at me five times at point blank range. I counted them!

Five shots, and all five bullets went into the ground between my feet.

The hitchhiker looked kind of puzzled. He backed off, reloaded his gun, and said, "Start walking."

I walked out into the cornfield, saying, "Greater is He that is in me than he that is in the world (1 John 4:4) ...the Word of God works...I have authority over the enemy!"

After we had walked about a hundred and fifty yards, he said, "Take your clothes off!"

FAITH ALWAYS WINS
· · ·

I did, and there I stood — God's man of faith and power — in a cornfield in Mexico in my underwear. But I was winning! When he saw that he could not kill me, he decided to rob me. He took my clothes; and, with my car keys in his hand, he turned around and walked off, fully intending to get into my car and drive away.

I said, "God, I have done what Your Word says to do. I have operated in the Word of God, not in the flesh. I have taken authority over the devil. I have done everything the Word says. Now, either Your Word works, or it does not. I believe it works. If it does not, I am not going to pay any attention to it anymore. I will just throw it away. But I believe that it works. It has kept me from being killed — but he cannot rob me either! And he fully intends to get into my car."

When he was about twenty yards from my car, I said, "God, this is not one of those times when I need an answer day after tomorrow. I need an answer right now!"

Then I yelled at the man, "I charge you in the name of Jesus to come back here!"

The man did not even break stride as he made a 180-degree turn and came back to where I was standing!

He threw my clothes at me and said, "Put them on!"

As I put my clothes back on, he yelled, "What is it that you wanted to talk to me about?"

He acted as if I had made an appointment with him.

"MI CASA ES SU CASA"
. . .

"I do not want to talk to you about anything else. I am telling you that I am a man of God. You have found out that you cannot rob or kill me. I am going home."

They have a saying in Mexico: "Mi casa es su casa," which means, "My house is your house."

I said, "If you want to go home with me, I will help you in any way possible. But we are not playing your game anymore."

He shook his head and said, "You know, I like you!"

He put his gun in his belt as he said, "I am going to put my confidence in you."

However, when we got to the car, he took out his gun again and said, "I am going to drive. You sit in the back."

"No!" I told him. "I am a man of God. I have authority in this situation. You cannot do anything. I have all the authority in the name of Jesus. It is my car, and I am going to drive. You can go or stay here. Now, give me my keys, in Jesus' name."

The man handed me my keys. We got into my car and drove off. I told him that Jesus came to earth to die for him, was resurrected for him, and is sitting on the right hand of the Father making intercession for him.

We came to a little place called Jalpa, about halfway between Zacatecas and Guadalajara.

He said, "I cannot go to Guadalajara with you. Take me up into the mountains. I have some friends up in the Sierras."

I consented to do this. He showed me where to turn off, and we made our turn right into three policemen, leaning against a police car in front of the police station.

He pulled his gun out and said, "Do not do anything, or I will kill you first, and then as many policemen as I can before they kill me."

I said, "What do I need policemen for? I have the name of Jesus."

"Oh, yeah," he said, as he put his gun back up. We drove up into the mountains for about thirty miles.

Finally, I stopped and said, "Look, I cannot take you any farther. I just have enough gas to get to Guadalajara, and I have given you all my money ($2). I would give you more if I had it. I only have enough gas to get home, so I am going home. You can either get out, or you can go home with me."

"I will get out," he said.

I gave him some food and some other things I had brought from Houston. He reached into his pockets and pulled out my watch, rings, and all the other things he had taken from me.

"You can have that," I said.

"You are giving them to me?"

I said, "You cannot take them from me. You cannot rob me. Just give me my wedding ring, and you can have my other rings, my watch, and all the other stuff. Now, I will pray for you before you get going."

I laid my hands on the hitchhiker and prayed for him. I told him where he could find me if he ever wanted to, and as I drove away toward Guadalajara and my family, he was walking up into the mountains.

That night, I am sure the man sat up there in the mountains, looking at his gun, and wondering why he was not a rich man. The equipment I had with me cost thousands of dollars in the United States, and three times that price in Mexico. He could have been a wealthy man.

A gun is supposed to represent power and authority, according to the world's thinking. But the authority of God's Word is real power! The Word of God works, and I get excited about it.

I am glad that it is life to those who find it. (Proverbs 4:20-22.) If it had not been life to me, or if I had not found it, the buzzards would have picked my bones out there in that cornfield. Those five bullets would have done me in.

I thank God for His Word! It is life to those that find it and health, or medicine, to their flesh. (Proverbs 4:22.) God honors His Word. He shows Himself strong on our behalf when we operate in His Word. (2 Chronicles 16:9.)

GOD IS NO RESPECTER OF PERSONS
• • •

Some time after my experience with the hitchhiker, I was attending a Kenneth Hagin Campmeeting in Tulsa, Oklahoma, when a girl came running up to me and asked, "Are you Terry Mize?"

"Yes, I am," I said.

"I have been asking God if I could meet you," she said.

I thought, "You have to be kidding. Why would anyone want to meet me? Why should anyone ask God if she could meet *me?*"

She said, "John Osteen came to Rhema Bible Training Center in Broken Arrow, Oklahoma, and shared your hitchhiker testimony."

I said, "Well, praise God!"

She went on, "That night when I left Rhema and went home, there was a man in my apartment. He had taken his clothes off and was going to attack me. When I walked in and turned on the lights, there he was. I just froze.

"Then I thought of the testimony Brother Osteen had just given. I thought, 'If that guy Brother Osteen was talking about could do it, I can do it, too.'

"So I started rebuking him in the name of Jesus. He turned around, walked back into the bathroom, put his clothes on, walked past me, opened the door, and left."

That is the reason she wanted to meet me. Thank God, the Word of God works! You are walking around with the unlimited power of the God of the universe inside you. Yet most Christians are sitting in their churches, on their blessed assurance, not doing anything with the power within them. There is world-overcoming power in God's Word, and in you. It is up to each one of us to do something about it.

When I Got the Message
· · ·

God began to show me parts of the faith message in 1967 when I was only seventeen. I preached my first sermon then on "you can have what you say."

I started out with Mark 11:23 and then went to Genesis where God created the world with His Word. I went to the book of Joshua where he stopped the sun and moon with words. I shared how God told Moses to get water out of a rock with words.

"Throughout the Old and New Testaments, you can read where God created everything with His Word," I told the congregation.

Jesus spoke to inanimate objects, and they obeyed Him. (Mark 4:39.) He spoke to dead men, and they came back to life. (John 11:43.) He spoke to demons, and they obeyed Him. (Mark 5, Luke 8.) He spoke to sick men, and they were healed. (John 5.)

My delivery was not too good when I first started preaching, but the message was good. However, some older Christians told me that message was not right, so I put it on the shelf and did not go on with it. Then I found through personal experience that the message had been correct after all, and those experienced Christians had been wrong.

About four years after preaching that sermon, I was in the Army. One day, I was out on the firing range checking out some weapons. I was firing a 45-caliber pistol, and I could not hit anything with it. Some people can hit a target with a .45, but I never could. Then I did a stupid thing: I brought up my other arm, laid the barrel of the gun across my forearm to brace it close to my face, and fired.

That pistol is not made to fire close to your face; it is made to fire at arm's length. So it damaged my ear drums. It is natural for one's ears to ring on the firing range, but my ears did not stop ringing. They continued to ring and ring and ring. That went on for days, then weeks, then into months — twenty-four hours a day. My ears never stopped ringing. It was a terrible thing — day and night.

I began to lose my hearing. Jackie would ask me if I could hear certain sounds, but I could not. Once when we were in a restaurant in El Paso, Texas, a man walked by wearing cowboy boots and spurs. Jackie asked me if I heard his spurs. I turned around, looked at him, and saw his spurs going up and down, but I could not hear them jingling. Certain sounds were not audible to me.

At that time we did not know much about faith and confession, and we were both confessing that I was going "deaf." Jackie would ask me if I could hear a certain sound, and I would answer, "No, I can't hear that." Then she would tell me that I was going deaf. I would agree and say, "Yes, I'm going deaf."

WHO IS THE LIAR?
. . .

Finally, it dawned on me that I would have to do something concerning my healing, or I would go deaf. I knew God healed. There was no problem with my knowledge. I took a three-day pass from the Army and went to a town in West Texas where a friend of mine, Tommy Williams, was pastoring a church. He has a good healing ministry.

When I arrived at his church, I asked him to pray for me because I was going deaf. He laid hands on me and prayed. He did everything he was supposed to do, and nothing happened. I left there with my ears ringing the same as they were when I arrived.

The next day, as I was driving around by myself before returning to El Paso, I asked the Lord, "How come for years I have been praying for people, and they get healed; yet I got prayed for, and I did not get healed?"

The Lord answered, "Son, one of us is a liar."

I said, "What did You say?"

"Me or you — one of us is a liar," He said.

I said, "I don't understand."

The Lord said, "*Your* word says you got prayed for and were not healed. *My* Word says you were healed by the stripes of Jesus. (1 Peter 2:24.) One of us is a liar. Either My Word is not any good, or your word is not any good. One of us is a liar."

I said, "My Lord! I see that, but I do not understand it. If I asked my ears if they were healed, they would say, 'No' because they are still ringing. But You say that they are healed. The Almighty God of the universe says they

25

are healed. If God says I am healed, then I must be healed. I do not understand that. I do not feel healed, I do not look healed, but if You say I am healed, then I must be healed. If the Almighty God of the universe says I am healed, then who am I to say I am not? I must be healed, for God says I am healed."

I began to confess that in the car, and I made this promise to God:

"Father, I make a vow unto You that, from this day forward, I will make my words agree with Your Words on every subject — whether it is my marriage, my children, my ministry, my finances, or my healing. Whatever it is, I will force my words to agree with Your Word. If I do not know what Your Word says about a situation that arises, I will go to Your Word and look it up. I will find out what Your Word says about it, and that is what I will say. I will make myself agree with You.

All the way back to El Paso, I said, "I am healed. The Word of God says I am healed, so I must be healed. By the stripes of Jesus I am healed."

My ears were still ringing and felt no different.

THE PRAYER OF AGREEMENT
· · ·

When I arrived in El Paso, I told Jackie that my ears were healed.

"Oh!" she said, "Did they stop ringing?"

I said, "That is none of your business. God says they are healed, and if God says they are healed, then they must be healed."

Jackie just looked at me and said, "I will agree with that."

Praise God for a wife who will agree with you. She did not argue with me or say, "You know you are not healed. You still cannot hear!"

She simply said, "I will agree with that."

We had Mark 11:23 working for us: "You can have what you say."

We also had Matthew 18:19 working for us: **If two of you shall agree on earth as touching any thing that they shall ask, it shall be done for them of my Father which is in heaven.**

We kept saying and agreeing that I was healed. In three days I realized that my healing had manifested completely!

Since that time, I have become an airplane pilot, so I have a physical and have my ears checked every year. Every time they check my ears, they find I have perfect hearing. Praise God!

I got a revelation that day of what I now live, preach, and believe every day. It has worked for me since the day I acted on God's Word and began to speak His Word on the subject. From that day to this, I have made my words agree with God's Word.

People thought then, and some still think, that I am crazy. They branded me "a nut" because they could not see in the natural what was actually going on. People came to our house and made fun of us.

FOOLISHNESS TO THE WORLD
· · ·

One lady came to visit, and when I let her in, she said, "Yea, yea; nay, nay."

I said, "What did you say?"

She repeated, "Yea, yea; nay, nay."

"What are you talking about?" I asked.

"I hear that all you can say over here is 'Yea, yea; nay, nay.'"

I was not quite that bad, but I did not want any unbelief spoken in my house. Jackie and I were struggling to make ourselves come in line with the Word of God, and we did not want anybody bringing any unbelief into our house.

I can tell you beyond a shadow of a doubt that God's Word works! Just say, and mean, what the Word of God has to say, and God will back it up. He will not back up what *you* say, but He will back up what *He* says. When you say what God says, then you are in business. Christians do not have to have lightning-fast minds to realize that they can agree with God.

Most Christians do not shake their fists at heaven and say, "God, You are a liar."

But in so many words that is what they are doing when they say things like, "I know Your Word says I am healed: but I am sick, I hurt, I have pain. Yes, Lord, I know Your Word says my finances are met and my needs are taken care of, but there is no money in the bank. The bills are piled high."

In so many words they tell God they know what His Word says, but His Word must not be true because of their situation.

The smartest thing I ever did, and the smartest thing you can ever do, is to agree with God. God has been around much longer than us, and He knows more than we do. He has seniority over the whole bunch of us!

He built this place, He invented the rules, and He can make things go the way He wants them to go. He knows best what to do to make things work and how they work. It makes good sense on our part to believe God.

If God said it, that settles it, whether you believe it or not.

Many people base the Word of God on their experiences. We must base our experiences on the Word of God.

C H A P T E R 3

Filling Up on the Word

I first went to the mission field when I was eighteen. Actually, I had studied Spanish in Mexico when I was fifteen, because God had told me two years earlier that I was going to the mission field.

However, I went on my first missionary trip when I was eighteen. I went to live with the Choco Indians in the jungles of Panama.

On that first trip, I saw "empty" missionaries everywhere I went. That bothered me, and I said to God:

"Lord, there are two things that bother me — one is 'empty' missionaries, and the other is people getting saved, but then being left with no follow-up care available."

God answered me and said, "Well, son, when you go out full time, you pour out, and pour out, and pour out. Then you must return to the States, go to meetings, and fill up."

When we went on the mission field full time, we made sure that follow-up care *was* made available to our converts wherever we were. Also, we made sure that once back in the States, we attended meetings to get refilled.

However, most missionaries conduct their ministry on a different basis. They minister in the country to which they are called, then they come back to the States and work as hard as they did on the field.

They itinerate, raising money for whatever it is they are doing on the field. They are constantly pouring out, but never filling up.

When they go back to the mission field, they end up with hepatitis or some other sickness, and many times, have to return home burned out for God.

But God told me to go to the mission field and minister, then come back and fill up.

He said, "Do not ever itinerate or raise money. I will supply the finances. You just fill up."

Every time I come back to the States, I go to a Kenneth Hagin meeting or a Kenneth Copeland meeting — or other churches or places where I know I can get fed — and I just soak up the Word.

Many times Jackie and I have driven ten hours one way to be in a John Osteen meeting in Houston. We were hungry for the Word, and it was always worth it.

MISSIONARIES NEED PRAYER
• • •

If you go to all the little prayer meetings in your town, you will find that some of them are nothing more than "bless-me clubs." Go to the services at all the churches in town, and listen to the prayer requests. Most of them are based on "me."

You seldom hear anybody say, "Let's pray for the world. Let's pray for missions. Let's pray for the missionaries in China and the Christians in Russia."

It is always, "Lord, bless me. Bless my uncle, my sister, my ingrown toenail. Pray for me. Pray for my finances and my headache."

Jesus cannot come back for the Church until we tell the world about Him. We need to be concerned about the world. Jesus was concerned enough about it to die for it. When most missionaries fulfill speaking engagements, they invariably come in with slide projectors under their arms and their hands out. They are stereotyped, because that is the picture the world has of missionaries.

I do not want to look like a "typical" missionary.

Many people say to my wife or me, "You do not look like missionaries."

We just say, "Thank you."

I must admit, however, there have been a few times when I felt like a "typical" missionary:

When I was in the jungles of Guatemala, eating monkey meat and fish eyeballs, or when it was 115 degrees in the shade, and there was no air-conditioning. Sometimes I do feel like a missionary, but I do not ever want to present that attitude.

WHOSE FAULT IS IT?
• • •

The Church has made the missionary what he is today. Christians in the States have set the pattern and the mold. They have made him drive his old car, wear his "holey" shoes and slick pants, and stand on the outside edges of the crowd with his hand out. The missionary fits that pattern, and it is the fault of the Church. But I have set out to do something about it.

I want to change the world's attitude about missionaries. Jesus was a missionary: He came and told this world about Himself. Whether you know it or not, whether you like it or not, as a Christian, you are a missionary.

Jesus said, **Go ye into all the world.** (Mark 16:15). Well, the "world" may be your next-door neighbor, or the person you work with, as well as people in the uttermost parts of the earth. *You* are supposed to go to the world. God has called every one of His children to be a missionary. You are either a "goer" or a "sender," but you are a missionary. There is no way you can get out of that divine calling.

I used to ask God, "Father, just let me be a 'sender.' I will make money and send it to missions around the world."

But God said, "No, Terry, you are a 'goer.'"

Of course, now Jackie and I are both "senders" and "goers." We have money invested around this globe in many countries, and we are excited about doing it.

MOUNTAINTOP OR VALLEY?
• • •

I was reared in a Christian home. In my home church the people were filled with the Spirit and knew the reality of the power of the Holy Spirit. There were even healings and miracles taking place. I was excited about that, but then I began to look at how people were living.

If the preacher had a good sermon on Sunday night, they were all on the mountaintop. There was glory, shouting, hand clapping, and foot stomping! Everyone was excited about God!

However, along came Monday morning. The bills were due. They had to go to work. Problems confronted them, and they started downhill, heading towards the valley. It was either the mountaintop or the valley. That was all I heard, and I was like the rest of them. About half my prayers were answered, which was about par for the course for everyone else.

Then I began to get hold of the Word of God. I always believed that if God's Word said it, it was so. So Jackie and I began to get excited about God's Word. Since that time, we have put it into practice for ourselves.

When I was in the Army is when I first began to see that Christians were not gaining victory in their lives but only having a measure of success. Then I saw in the Word of God what the Lord said to Joshua after Moses died when Joshua became leader of Israel:

> **This book of the law shall not depart out of thy mouth; but thou shalt meditate therein day and night, that thou mayest observe to do according to all that is written therein: for then thou shalt make thy way prosperous, and then thou shalt have good success.**
>
> **Joshua 1:8**

Everyone wants to prosper and have good success. When I saw what worked for Joshua, I decided to put it into practice for myself. I began to check out some of the other men in the Bible and saw that meditating in the

35

Word worked for them. I found that if you will meditate in the Word of God day and night, night and day, until it becomes a part of you, the Word will just roll around on the inside of you and then begin to squirt out your mouth — and you will have good success.

Jesus said whatever you inject into your heart — whatever you put in your heart in abundance — will come out your mouth. (Luke 6:45.) That principle is not just something good that Jesus said: It is a spiritual law. It works! If you do not believe that, the next time you hit your thumb with a hammer, just listen to what comes out of your mouth. It will be whatever is in you in abundance!

Jackie and I decided to get into the Word of God, to meditate those things night and day, day and night. A friend gave us a big blue book by Kenneth E. Hagin called *The Bible Faith Study Course.*[1] That was the best investment my friend ever made in his life. I would sit up and read that book to my wife until three or four a.m.

Jackie will tell you that is the one thing that got us to Mexico.

The Word was what we had going on the inside of us, filling us. We read that book day and night, night and day. We listened to tapes and read the Word of God. I am telling you: The Word of God works! It is the greatest thing I have ever had!

---

[1]Hagin, Kenneth E., *The Bible Faith Study Course,* 1972 edition; published by Kenneth E. Hagin Ministries, Tulsa, Oklahoma.

The Word of God works in Africa. It works in India. It works in Mexico. It works in Central America. It works in the States. People have told me that it will not work on the mission fields. Bless God, it works around the world! If it will not work in Africa, it will not work anywhere.

I am excited about the Word of God. If it did not meet my needs, pay my bills, keep me well, and keep food on the table for the kids, I would not be nearly as excited about it as I am. I am turned on to the Word of God because it works!

People hear about different things we have done. They see us on different Christian television programs. They hear other ministers talking about us, and they think we are really special, "spiritual hotshots."

I want you to know that the Word of God works for anyone who works it. Testimonies do not produce the Word; the Word produces testimonies. Testimonies *inspire* faith; the Word *creates* faith.

I am invited to many Full Gospel Businessmen's Fellowship International chapter meetings and conventions to share my testimony about the hitchhiker. I have been a member of FGBMFI since I was sixteen and have helped set up chapters and conventions in foreign countries. I thank God for this organization that is reaching out to the whole world with the Gospel. But I always share the Word with my testimony, just as in this book, because then my testimony will both inspire *and* create faith.

The only special thing I have done is put the Word in first place. Without the Word, the testimony will never work. I would have been dead by now and singing in the heavenly choir if the Word had not worked!

Believe me, I have had many opportunities to go to heaven, but I have decided to stay — and I suggest that as you read this, you decide to stay too. Let us get the job done that Jesus told us to do.

God Confirms His Word
· · ·

When I first went to Mexico as a missionary, I had a wife and a two-year-old baby. We had zero means of monthly support, and no one cared that we were going to the mission field. Not many people even knew we were going. The only mission board we had then is the same one we have today: The Father, Son, and Holy Ghost. That is a good mission board!

Contrary to what you may have heard, the cost of living in Mexico is higher than it is in the United States. When we left, there was only one church that was supposed to support us. They had said they would send us $100 a month, but they did not.

We did not know anybody and did not know what to do. The one contact we had was a lady who said we could go into the country with her. I had gone to Mexico with her before, but as we were ready to leave, she died.

We had temptations, testings, and trials. We had many opportunities not to go to Mexico. But we had made a quality decision that we were going! Jackie and I also made another quality decision: to have one campaign a month.

We said, "In the name of Jesus, we are having one campaign in Latin America or somewhere in the world every month."

For years, we have had a campaign every month! We have not even considered canceling one of them. It does not enter our minds to do so, because we set our faith to do it, and that is what we have been doing.

We are excited about what God is doing. If His Word did not work, I would not go on the mission field; but the Word does work and it turns me on! God said that His Word would make you successful and make you prosperous.

Proverbs 4:20 says: **My son, attend to my words; incline thine ear unto my sayings.**

That does not mean to casually glance at His Word once in a while. No good Christian home is completely decorated without a fifteen-pound Bible on the coffee table. But unless you do something with the Word — get it inside you — it will never do you any good.

Let us say I went off on a trip, and my neighbor agreed to tend to my yard while I was gone; but, when I came back I found the grass unkempt and up to my knees. Nothing had been taken care of.

Then my neighbor came over and said, "Well, Terry, I came by and looked at your yard every day."

He did not attend to my lawn; he just *looked* at it. God said, "Attend to My Word. *Attend* to it." We look at the Bible and talk about how holy it is. We enshrine it in a glass case and religiously dust it off. We can have a thousand Bibles in our homes; but, until we get that Word inside us, they will not do any good. We have to attend to the Word.

ATTEND TO THE WORD
· · ·

Why did God tell us to incline our ears to His sayings? Because **faith cometh by hearing, and hearing by the word of God** (Romans 10:17).

Let not *what* depart? Those words, those sayings. Do not let the sayings of God depart from your eyes. Keep them in the midst of your heart, because they are life.

The Word should be taken like medicine. If you hurt three times a day, take the Word three times a day. If you need to take it ten times a day, take it ten times a day. Take the Word as often as necessary, just like medicine. Get the Word of God inside you and make it work for you.

When Jesus was being tempted by Satan, He made this statement to him: **It is written, That man shall not live by bread alone, but by every word of God** (Luke 4:4).

Jesus was saying the same thing that Proverbs 4:22 says: The words of God are life to those who find them.

God said in Jeremiah 1:12: ...**I will hasten my word to perform it.** He will watch over His Word to see that it comes true.

David said in Psalm 138:2: ...**thou hast magnified thy word above all thy name.** For God to deny His Word, He would have to deny His name. God takes great stock in His Word. You can base your life on the Word of God. You can base anything on His Word.

I know a Mexican pastor who is a tremendous man of faith, although you will probably never hear of him until you get to heaven.

He says, "Faith is like being up on a high diving board, beginning to bounce, and diving off — knowing full well that, as your feet leave the diving board, there is no water in the pool — but believing that God will fill the pool with water before you get there."

I have never found faith to work for me until I moved out on it.

This pastor also says, "Faith is like painting a two-story building. While you are painting, the ladder falls out from under you. There you hang by the paint brush, but you just keep on painting!"

He is a man of faith!

God said in Jeremiah 32:27: **Behold, I am the Lord, the God of all flesh: is there any thing too hard for me?**

I constantly remind Him: "No, Sir, there is nothing too hard for You."

BLAMING IT ALL ON GOD
• • •

Acts 10:38 says:

How God anointed Jesus of Nazareth with the Holy Ghost and with power: who went about doing good, and healing all that were oppressed of the devil; for God was with him.

This scripture tells me several things: God is good, Jesus is good, the Holy Ghost is good, and the devil is bad.

GOD CONFIRMS HIS WORD

Some people act as if the devil is doing the good stuff, and God is doing the bad stuff. That is not correct.

I am a pilot. Once I was in an airplane hangar in South Texas and saw a big sign on the back of the hangar: "We are not responsible for fire, theft, or other acts of God."

I went to the guy who worked there and said, "Fellow, I do not know who your god is, but mine does not act that way. My God does not set fire to airplanes, and my God does not steal airplanes. What do you mean, 'other acts of God'?"

He said, "Well, you know, anything we can't explain."

Anything we cannot explain, anything tragic, we blame on God. Even insurance companies classify as "an act of God" anything they cannot explain, or do not want to pay for. Why do they not tell the truth and say the devil did it? He is the one doing all of it.

Remember the lady in Luke 13 who had been bowed over for eighteen years and could in no wise lift herself up?

Jesus did not say, "Oh, hallelujah! Look what God has done!"

No. He said, "Shouldn't this daughter of Abraham be loosed from the bondage of Satan?" (Luke 13:16.)

Then He healed her.

The Word says that she immediately glorified God. (Luke 13:13.) She glorified God for the healing. God is a good God!

Most people have such immature ideas of God. Some people picture God as an old man sitting on His throne. He has a long white beard and a wart on the end of His nose. There is a big stick in His hand, and whenever you move, He goes *blap!*

No! My God is a good God. He is my Father. God is love, and He loves us. We read in 2 Chronicles 16:9:

> **For the eyes of the Lord run to and fro throughout the whole earth, to shew himself strong in the behalf of them whose heart is perfect toward him.**

I say, "That's me, God. You do not have to look any farther. Your eyes are running to and fro, looking for someone You can show Yourself strong to. Here I am!"

As I was praying one time in Mexico, God showed me a scripture in the 11th chapter of Matthew, where John the Baptist sent two of his disciples to Jesus.

THE MINISTRY OF JESUS
• • •

He said, "Go over there and ask Jesus if He is the One who is to come, or should we look for another?"

Jesus replied, "You go back and tell John the things that you have seen and heard. You have seen the blind see, the deaf hear, the lame walk, the devils cast out, the lepers cleansed, and the Gospel preached to the poor." (Matthew 11:4,6.)

As I was reading that, I began to cry and say, "God, that is what I want — the ministry of Jesus."

That is what every believer should aim for.

Since that time, we have had every one of those miracles happen in our ministry. We have had the dead raised. We see blind eyes opened on a constant basis. The deaf hear in every campaign. We see devils cast out. Even lepers have been healed.

Jesus listed these things in Mark 16 in their order of simplicity. The first thing He said was that believers will cast out devils. He listed the easiest things first.

We have made the devil seem so big, bad, and powerful, but he is not. Jesus said believers will cast out devils in His name. Casting out devils is no big deal. We have devils cast out of every demon-possessed person in every service.

There is much teaching going on in the United States about deliverance. Thank God for the deliverance ministry. It is a valid ministry, but it is very misused and abused. In the States, we usually do not have demon-possessed people in our services. Most of them are either in institutions or can be readily spotted — the guy on top of the building with a sniper's rifle, shooting everybody.

In many communities in third world nations, however, you could see a man who has been chained to a tree for fifteen or twenty years, because he is demon-possessed. In almost every campaign, we have to deal with at least one case, and sometimes many cases, of demon possession.

I remember one little nine-year-old boy in particular. In reform school, they would chain him down — spread-eagle, hands and feet — and he would break those chains. I prayed for him, and God set him free!

You say what God said, and you preach what Jesus said. God is not going to confirm what I think He said or what some other preacher thought He said. God is going to confirm His Word — what *He* has said.

One time, God spoke to me and said, "Read me the last verse of Mark 16."

I said, "I have been able to quote verses 15-20 since I was a little kid. It says, **Go ye into all the world....** Verse 19 says that Jesus ascended into heaven and sits on the right hand of the Father.

He said. "Read it."

I read verses 19 and 20:

> **So then after the Lord had spoken unto them, he was received up into heaven, and sat on the right hand of God.**
>
> **And they went forth, and preached every where, the Lord working with them, and confirming the word with signs following.**

It was such a relief to me to realize that all I had to do was go everywhere and preach. I was not working for God, and God was not working for me. God was working *with* me, confirming His Word with signs following. I did not have to make the signs. My job was to go everywhere and preach.

God gladly and readily confirms His Word with signs following. That is what we do, and that is what we have been doing: preaching the Word and trusting God to confirm it. Every campaign is just like the previous one. God confirms His Word with signs following.

Is It God or the Devil?
· · ·

John 10:10 is one of my favorite scripture verses. It tells how you can know what is of God and what is of the devil. You do not have to have lightning flashes, thunder rolls, and goose bumps to know what is of God.

Jesus said:

> **The thief cometh not, but for to steal, and to kill, and to destroy: I am come that they might have life, and that they might have it more abundantly.**
>
> **John 10:10**

It is as simple as that. Anything that has to do with stealing, killing, or destroying is of the devil. It is not God and has nothing to do with God. Anything that has to do with life and abundance is Jesus.

I can recognize Him anywhere! I do not have to go off somewhere and pray to know whether or not cancer is of God. It is stealing. If something is destroying your home and your marriage, robbing your finances, robbing your health, and bringing death, it is Satan. Run him off!

You do not have to get some divine revelation to know what is of God and what is of the devil. Just as plain as can be, Jesus said, "If it is killing, stealing, or destroying, it is of the devil. If it brings life and abundance, it is Me. That is My calling card."

Once we were having an open-air campaign in Honduras, and twenty-five thousand people were coming to the meetings. I had finished one of the morning meetings and was wrapping up the microphone and getting ready to go inside for the rest of the day. It is 110 degrees there in February.

A lady came up on the platform, crying. She was expecting a baby and was several months along.

She said, "Brother, I've not felt my baby move for days. I'm bleeding profusely, and I'm in a lot of pain. I've been to the doctor, and he says the baby is dead. He wants me to go to the hospital, so he can take it from me."

I turned to her and said, "Sister, a dead baby on the inside of you is not life in abundance. It is killing, stealing, and destroying. It is not God. I decree, as a man of God, in the name of Jesus that your baby will live and not die. Now, go back to the doctor."

The woman left. I looked for her each day, but did not see her. On the fourth day of the campaign, she came up in the prayer line. Her face was radiant! She gave her testimony before those thousands of people:

"When the brother prayed for me (actually, I did not pray for her; I just turned to her and spoke a statement of faith) the pain and the bleeding stopped. When I got back to the doctor's office, I felt the baby move. The doctor examined me and said that everything was perfect."

That is Jesus! I would recognize Him anywhere! That is life in abundance! I did not have to wonder what was of God and what was of the devil. All I have to do is operate the Word of God. He will confirm it with signs following!

Redeemed From the Curse
• • •

We have been redeemed from the curse of the Law. (Galatians 3:13; Deuteronomy 28.)

The opposite of the curse is true for us. Jesus reversed the curse! You can get a medical dictionary that lists every disease and write across the pages:

"I have been redeemed from that. None of those diseases are coming upon me or my family, because we have been redeemed from the curse of the Law."

While we were living in Mexico, I received a long distance call from home one day. When I said, "Hello," the hysterical voice of my aunt said, "Terry, you have to come home right now! Your grandmother is dying!"

I did not think about what to say. These words just came out of my mouth: "That is a lie right out of the pit of hell."

There was a man standing next to me at the phone, and all he heard me say was, "Hello. That is a lie right out of the pit of hell."

I am sure he wondered who in the world I was talking to!

I asked my aunt "Did you say she's dead, or she's dying?"

She answered, "She's dying. She is in the hospital and has only a 20 percent chance of making it. She has sugar diabetes."

I already knew that and had been trying to pump some faith into her so she could believe God for her healing, but she had not received it yet. She could not write, and she could not read our letters from Mexico because she was going blind.

My aunt went on, "She's getting worse. Her heart is weak and is failing. Her kidneys have totally stopped functioning. They have her under oxygen, and she is real swollen. She has a 20 percent chance of making it through the night, or for a few days at the most. You have to come home."

I said, "There is no way I can come home right now."

She said again, "But you *have* to come home."

"I'm not coming home," I told her.

That was the middle of April, and I could not go home until May. Jackie and I intended to go home for our anniversary, which was May 10th.

I said, "We are coming home on May 10th, and I'll tell you this: She *will* live. She will not die before I get home."

But I could not get that across to my aunt.

She said, "She's going to die."

I said, "No, she's not!"

I went to several prayer groups in Guadalajara and asked them to set their faith in agreement with me about my grandmother. The first thing they all wanted to know was how old she was.

I said, "It makes no difference how old she is. I say she is not going to die. You either agree with me or you do not."

So I set my faith and believed God. I arrested the spirit of death and commanded it to get out of her room. I spoke life to her and believed God for her. In three or four days, I called home for a report.

My aunt said, "Her kidneys have been functioning a little bit, but she's still going to die."

I said to her, "You don't seem to be listening to what I am telling you. She will live and not die. She will not die before I come home, and I'm coming home May 10th."

Then she said, "Well, I want Tommy Williams to preach at the funeral!"

I said, *"You're not hearing what I'm saying!* There is not going to be a funeral, because she is not going to die. I'm going to call Tommy Williams and tell him to get her out of the hospital, not preach at her funeral.

OUR WORDS CAN BE KILLERS
· · ·

My aunt was a Spirit-filled woman. However, she and the other members of the family would go over to the hospital, take Grandmother's hand, and say, "Now, Mother, you have lived a long life, and the Lord is taking you home."

Words like that are killers. We must watch what we say. You can be saved, filled with the Holy Ghost for fifty years, and still not know what the Word of God says.

I said, "Look, if you can't believe the Word of God — if you cannot do anything except take that negative junk up to the hospital — then stay home and watch television! Don't go up there and kill my grandmother. If you can't say anything else, then just say, 'Terry has arrested the spirit of death, and Terry says you will not die, in the name of Jesus.'"

I hung up the phone and did not talk to my aunt anymore. I handled it from a thousand miles away. I called Tommy Williams and had him go to the hospital to pray for her. But when time came for us to leave Mexico, I still could not get away. So Jackie and our son went alone. I told her to go to the hospital and take care of the situation.

On our anniversary I called and asked Jackie how things were going at the hospital.

She said, "Every time I go there and minister the Word of God, your grandmother is fine. Then someone goes in and tells her the Lord is taking her home, and she gets worse."

"Well, don't let them in there anymore. Run them off; slap them in the face; do anything you have to; but don't let them in there!"

Jackie said, "Terry, I can't do your relatives like that. You had better come home."

I left the next day to go home. Jackie picked me up at the airport, and we went directly to the hospital. All the way there, I kept saying, "Greater is He Who is in me than he who is in the world. She will live and not die."

Now what I did may sound hard, but I had to get my grandmother's attention. I could have sympathized with her and put her in a casket, but I did not want her to die. The difference between compassion and sympathy is that compassion does something. Jesus was moved with compassion.

I walked into that hospital and went straight to her room. Instead of saying hello to her, I got right to the point: "Do you want to die and go on to heaven to be with Jesus and Grandad? If you do, just help yourself. If you don't, then get into agreement with me. Get up out of that bed, go home, and cook me something to eat! That's where you ought to be in the first place!"

Grandmother started crying and said, "I don't want to die."

"That's all I wanted to know. Now, you say this after me: Christ has redeemed me from the curse of the Law. Sugar diabetes is under the curse. Kidney problems are under the curse. Therefore, I don't have any of that. I'm healed in the name of Jesus."

She repeated it after me. I had her say it again and again, all day and all night. I did not pray for her. I wanted her faith to get to work.

Sometimes we pray for people too quickly. What heals? **He sent his word, and healed them** (Psalms 107:20). His *Word* healed them.

GOD'S WORD HEALS
. . .

I can pray and run off the biggest devil, but when I leave, unless the person keeps that devil away, he will be back. If I put the Word of God into a person, then run off the devil, he will not be able to come back. I do not pray for people without giving them some instruction, because I know that most people will not be able to keep their healings otherwise.

I have seen demon-possessed people to whom I could have ministered deliverance — but I knew that when I left, that devil would come back. The Bible says if he comes back and finds the house swept and garnished, he will come in and bring seven more worse than himself. I do not want to leave those people in a worse state, so I put the Word of God in them first, then I run off the devil. If he comes back and finds that house full of the Word of God, he will go on to "easier pickings."

I gave my grandmother that confession and told her to say it, and say it, and say it. Then I told her I believed she was in good shape and I needed to go to Oklahoma, so I left.

Four days later she got up and went home!

Her doctor told her, "I don't understand it, but you don't have to take insulin anymore for that sugar diabetes."

After she went home, I prayed, "Lord, I don't want her kidneys healed; I want her kidneys replaced. They are 73 years old, and I want brand new ones."

The Lord gave her brand new kidneys that function perfectly. However, a year or so after that, she got into trouble again with her health. Grandmother went to the doctor who told her that her husband had died of heart trouble, she had a history of heart trouble, so she too would die of heart trouble. When my mother told me that,

I decided to wait a couple of days, then call Grandmother. She would be starting to hurt by then.

When I called her, I asked, "How are you today?"

I usually do not ask how people are feeling because I do not want to hear it.

She said, "I don't feel too good, Terry. When I took out the garbage this morning, I had a slight heart attack. My heart is hurting me. I went to the doctor last Friday, and he told me I would continue to have trouble."

"Why don't you just go ahead and die?"

She said, "What?"

I repeated, "Why don't you just go ahead and die? That's what you are working for."

"Terry, what are you talking about?"

I said, "I'll tell you what I'm talking about. You went to the doctor feeling totally fine, but he told you that you were going to die of heart trouble. You believed his word, and faith comes by hearing. Then you told all four of your daughters, and probably every neighbor you could possibly tell and now you're telling me.

"You have just set into motion two spiritual laws. You can have Mark 11:23 working for you, or against you. You can have whatever you say with your mouth. You believe in your heart and are saying with your mouth that you have heart trouble, so that is exactly what you are going to have.

"You also have the spiritual law of Matthew 18:19 working for you, or against you. If any two of you agree on earth, it shall be so. You have all four of your daughters, plus your neighbors, agreeing with you. Now you are trying to get me to agree that you are going to die.

"Because you have these two spiritual laws working for you, it shouldn't take long to finish you off."

When she saw what she had done, I said, "Well, let's straighten it out. What did you do to get healed when you were in the hospital dying?"

She told me, "I said, 'Christ redeemed me from the curse; therefore, I do not have any of that stuff!'"

"That's right. So what are you going to do about this heart situation?"

"I'm going to say that Christ has redeemed me from the curse. Heart trouble is under the curse, and I'm not going to have heart trouble!"

Her pains went away! Praise God! I love my grandmother. I did not want to see her die, but I told her: "If you want to go be with the Lord, there is nothing wrong with that — but do not go sick. I will not hold you here, if you are tired and want to go. But I do not want you to go sick. If you go in pain, it is of the devil, not of God. If you want to go, then sit there in your easy chair and blast off!"

Grandmother stayed!

C H A P T E R   6

Jesus Makes House Calls
· · ·

As I was sitting in my office in Guadalajara one day, God spoke to me and told me to go back to the United States. He wanted me to learn to fly. Since then, He has had us traveling for Him, instead of working in only one town. It is more practical for us to live in the States and fly to different places every month, than it is to live in only one place in Mexico and do that.

While we were still living in Guadalajara, a lady came into my office one day. She was hysterical, crying and screaming: "My baby's dying! My baby's dying!"

I tried to calm her down and make some sense out of what she was saying in Spanish. Finally, I got her calmed down enough to talk to her. She said her nine-year-old daughter was in the military hospital in town dying of leukemia.

She said, "We have had her in three other hospitals in Guadalajara. The head of each hospital has given her up, with no hope, so we took her to the military hospital. This morning the head of that hospital gave her up, with no hope. She's dying! She's in pain, and nothing can be done!"

But I said, "Sister, the Word of God says that the thief comes to kill, steal, and destroy, but that Jesus has come to give you life, and that more abundantly. Your daughter dying of leukemia is not life in abundance; it is killing, stealing, and destroying. As a man of God, I say your baby will live and not die.

"Now, I would like to pray — not for your daughter, but for you to calm down so you can drive across town to the hospital."

Then I prayed for her and ministered to her.

She said, "Will you come to the hospital at 3 p.m.?"

"Yes," I said, "but your daughter is fine. She is healed. She will live and not die. But if it will make you feel better, I'll come to the hospital."

At 3 p.m., I walked into the hospital room, and the little girl was sitting up in bed playing. The parents and grandparents were talking, laughing, and visiting.

I said, "I thought she was sick!"

The grandmother said to me, "Brother, when the mother came into your office, my little granddaughter was in pain; nothing could be done for her. But while her mother was gone to your office, the little girl became as you see her now. There is nothing wrong with her! The doctors and nurses are amazed. They want to keep her for a week and run tests."

I said, "Fine. Let them keep her as long as they want to and run all the tests they want to run."

They kept the little girl a week and examined her. As they let her go home, they said, "She is cured of leukemia." That is life in abundance! That is Jesus.

Jesus Does Not Turn People Away
• • •

Once an American medical student came to me and said, "A girl that I know, a Mexican medical student, is dying with an incurable blood disease. They know what is wrong with her, but they can't cure it. She is in the hospital, dying. Will you come and pray for her?"

"Yes, I'll go," I replied.

I have always been impressed with the fact that Jesus is never too busy to make house calls. Remember the little lady with the issue of blood who came up and grabbed hold of His garment?

Jesus did not say, "Look, lady, I'm a busy evangelist. I've got a heavy appointment. Don't bother me."

Jesus always said, "Sure. I'll go."

When that medical student asked me to pray with the girl, I said, "Let's go!"

We went to the hospital ward where she was, but they would not let us pray for her. In the United States, a minister can walk into any hospital and pray for somebody. Not so in Mexico!

In the first place, it is illegal to be a missionary in Mexico.

It is illegal to preach the Gospel or give any kind of religious instruction in any building other than a church.

It is illegal to have home prayer meetings or hotel meetings, and it is illegal to pray for people in the hospital; I have had to fight my way through several hospitals in Mexico.

As I stood there in the ward, I could see that she was the worst-looking patient in the entire room. She looked like death. We needed to get the Word to her. I realize we could have prayed for her without laying hands on her, but I felt that I should get the Word to her. The Word heals.

The next day, we went back, but they still would not let us in, so we prayed, "God, You are going to have to do something to get us in there to minister Your Word to that girl, to minister life to her."

The Word of God is life to those who find it. By pumping the Word into people, you pump life into them. When you pray for people in faith, in the name of Jesus, there is not a devil or a sickness big enough that you cannot run off in Jesus' name.

If people do not have the Word in them, they have nothing to give them life. That spirit or that sickness will come back. We have seen this happen many times. But if you share the Word with somebody, that Word is life and medicine. It will work!

The next day, I went to the hospital again. When I looked into her ward, I saw that her bed was empty. The first thing the devil said to me was, "She died."

I found a nurse and asked, "What happened to the girl over there in that bed?"

She replied, "There's nothing that can be done for her, so the doctors sent her home to die."

"Praise God! I know what to do about that!" I said, as I hurried to my car.

JESUS ALWAYS MAKES A WAY
. . .

I drove across Guadalajara to the girl's home, went in, and shared the Word with her. Then I laid hands on her and prayed for her, in the name of Jesus. She was swollen and looked horrible; and I must say that when I finished praying for her, she did not look any different. But after I ministered the Word of God to her, I walked out of that place, believing that according to God's Word, she was healed by the stripes of Jesus.

The next Sunday, I was preaching at the center, and a beautiful girl walked in and sat down. I did not recognize her, but after the service, I found out that she was the girl I had prayed for. God's Word works! It will give you success. It will give you prosperity. It will give you life. It will heal your body.

I have preached and shared this word all across the United States and Latin America. Some people really receive it and do something with it. Others just say, "Yeah, that's nice."

Sometimes it's easier to deal with national pastors than with missionaries.

Missionaries say, "Look, we've been here seventy-two years. We know how it is, and what you are preaching won't work!"

A missionary once told me, "That stuff you are preaching would be nice, if I could believe it."

When I was in South Mexico, a missionary lady brought her daughter to me for prayer. She would not tell me what was wrong. She just said, "Pray for her." I laid hands on the little girl and prayed for her.

After the service, the mother said, "The doctor says she has a hernia and that it has to be surgically removed. You can see it, and you can feel it."

I said, "Well, I believe she is healed."

Then the missionary lady said, "Well, that's the trouble I've always had. I don't believe it."

"Well, I don't care if you believe it or not. I prayed for her, and I believe she was healed."

I found out later that the next day the lady's married daughter took off her little sister's clothes and examined her. There was no hernia there! She called her mother, showed her, and the mother agreed that the hernia was gone — but they never did give a testimony of it.

People will say, "Well, it's nice if you can believe it."

A Man Raised From the Dead
• • •

In 1976 while I was in Florida, Dr. Doug Fowler, a well-known surgeon in Jacksonville, invited me to share my testimony in his church on a Sunday morning. As I was sitting on the platform, about to take the pulpit, I saw a man there in the congregation who had the spirit of death upon him. Then he fell over dead.

Dr. Fowler ran over to him, took his pulse, listened to his heart, then said, "He's dead." An ambulance attendant in the church also said the man was dead. Everybody was standing up, trying to see what was going on, but I did not move. I just sat there, listening in my spirit.

Then the Spirit of the Lord spoke to me and said, "Go tell that man to let not his heart be troubled."

God will never tell you something that contradicts His Word. I knew that was the Word of God. Jesus said, **Let not your heart be troubled: ye believe in God, believe also in me** (John 14:1). We use that mostly at funerals, but God said, "Go tell him to let not his heart be troubled."

I made my way through the crowd to where the man was lying over in his seat, and I said to that dead man, "In the name of Jesus, don't let your heart be troubled."

Then I said, "I rebuke the spirit of death and command life to come back into you."

The man opened his eyes, shook his head, and got up. That is life in abundance! That is Jesus! I am not claiming any credit for that. Doug, the pastor, and the whole church were praying. All I did was obey God when He spoke to my heart. That was in July of 1976. When I went back there in March of 1977, I asked Dr. Fowler about that guy.

Doug said, "You know, he had never been to church before. He wasn't saved. He just walked into the service that morning, sat down, and died. But God raised him from the dead! If he had been in most churches, he would be spending eternity in hell. But he got saved, filled with the Holy Ghost, and is one of the most faithful workers in our church."

God told me to have a miracle service that night, so we did, and people were healed by the power of God. One thing that touched my heart was that Dr. Fowler's two little daughters (about ten years old) came up for prayer. The anointing of God was so strong that nobody could stand up. I was having to hold to the pulpit in order to stand. People had been seeing the power of God as a mist.

The two Fowler girls asked, "Would you pray for our grandmother? She was in a car wreck in December and has been in a coma for seven months."

I took their hands and, instantly, they went under the power of God. I held them up until I finished praying for their grandmother, then I just let them fall back under the power. After the service, the Fowlers took us out to eat. Doug was telling me that his mother had been in a car wreck and remained in a coma.

I said, "Well, Doug, God did something for her tonight. You will hear from this."

Bright and early the next morning, the phone rang in our motel room. It was Doug.

He said, "I just wanted to reach you before you left town. When we got home last night, there was a message waiting for us from the hospital that my mother was awake and normal."

That's Jesus!

God's Word Works!
· · ·

The Word of God is the most important thing you can get into your heart. If you inject the Word of God into your heart, it will create light, and you will be able to see that for which you are believing God.

Many times, when you are believing God for the desire of your heart, you cannot see it. Even though you are believing God for it, it is hard for you to picture it — hard for you to get hold of it. You need to inject God's Word into your heart, because the Word of God is light. It is a lamp unto your feet. (Psalms 119:105.)

Jesus is a light to us and to the world. (John 8:12.) We are also a light of the world. (Matthew 5:14.)

When we get God's Word in us, it will create light. We will be able to see into the spiritual world and see the desires of our hearts— the things for which we have been believing.

Jackie and I got excited about the Word of God a long time ago. We found that Jesus redeemed us from the curse of the Law. We found that we were redeemed from everything that was under the curse.

We decided that any kind of pain was under the curse, including pain of childbirth, so we started believing God. Jackie had three of our four children without any pain, anesthetic, stitches, or problems. We took God at His Word! (We did not know about these things when our first child was born.)

Supernatural Childbirth!
· · ·

Many women come to Jackie and say, "Oh, yeah, we did natural childbirth."

I am not talking about the world's "natural childbirth," about going to classes and learning how to breathe and pant. I am talking about believing the Word of God and giving birth without pain or problems, which is God's natural childbirth. I am not talking about having morning sickness. Morning sickness is under the curse of the Law.

It was a pleasure to live with Jackie when she was believing the Word of God during pregnancy. It was as though she was not even expecting a baby. She went around pleasantly, doing everything she was supposed to do. When the time came, she went into the hospital and had the baby.

We were living in Mexico at the time and did not know anyone else had done this. We were simply believing God. On a Saturday night, we believed that the baby should be born the next morning, so we stood on the Word of God.

We said, "God, we call You and Jesus and the Holy Ghost to record. We serve notice to all the angels and everybody in heaven, as well as to the devil and all his crew. We are going to read this to you because this is what we are believing."

Then we read Galatians 3:13: **Christ hath redeemed us from the curse of the law.**

We read from Genesis 3, where the curse was put on Eve, and we stated how the curse was removed by Jesus.

We read from Deuteronomy 28 about all the blessings and the curses.

Then we read 1 Timothy 2:15 that says women will be saved in childbearing.

We went back to the first chapter of Exodus and read where Pharaoh told all the midwives to kill every male baby that was born to the Hebrew women.

When Pharaoh found out that they had not been doing this, he called them in to find out why.

The midwives replied, "Those Hebrew women are not like Egyptian women. They are lively. They have their babies before we can get to them." (Exodus 1:19.)

The Hebrew women had a covenant with God. They were not like the Egyptian women, who had a hard time bearing children. Hebrew women had their babies without problems.

We read all of these Scripture passages to God, then said, "Now, Lord, this baby will be born in the morning. In Jesus' name, we thank You."

We got up the next morning and went to the hospital. Jackie began to have contractions. Her stomach muscles would contract, but there was no pain.

(Everybody talks about "labor pains." We decided not to call it "pain," because Jackie was not going to have any pain.)

When we walked into the hospital, we were laughing and talking, so they asked what we were doing there.

"I am going to have a baby," Jackie said.

"When are you going to have this baby?" they asked, because she was smiling and standing up without any outward pain.

"In ten minutes."

They laughed, and Jackie said, "I am not kidding you. I am going to have this baby now."

When we finally convinced them that she was serious, they checked her over, and all of them panicked!

Jackie had the baby in twenty minutes. She missed it by ten minutes. The baby, a boy, weighed ten pounds. During the delivery, Jackie had no pain, no anesthetic, and no problems.

After that, she had two more babies without pain or problems. One of them was born in Odessa, Texas.

When one of the nurses came in at that hospital, Jackie said, "Well, I am ready to have the baby."

The nurse said, "No. honey, I've been doing this a long time. Your smile has to change first. I know when a lady is about to have a baby, and your face has got to change! You're smiling."

Jackie said, "But I smile all the way through," and she did!

Ladies, if you are going to have a baby, you can do it without pain. Just get into the Word of God, and get the

Word down inside you. Then speak what God says in His Word about the situation.

THE WORD OF A KING
· · ·

During a campaign in Tepeapulco, Mexico, I was preaching "You Can Have What You Say." (Mark 11:23.) I showed them where the Word says we are kings and priests unto God (Revelation 1:6), and where Ecclesiastes 8:4 says, **Where the word of a king is, there is power.** I preached the Word, and we had some miracles. God was confirming His Word.

In Tepeapulco, there is a vehicle plant named Dina. When International Harvester Company quit making the Travelall and International pickup, they sold that part of their company to Mexico. Mexico now makes International pickups and calls them Dinas. The people make good wages at this plant.

The day after we started our evangelistic campaign, some people came to me and said, "The Dina plant is going to shut down Wednesday morning. The union has said so. They already have the placards made. The president of Mexico has said nothing can be done."

I went into the service that night and said, "Let me see the hands of those who will be affected if the Dina plant shuts down."

They all raised their hands.

"All right, last night I preached that where the word of a king is, there is power. I certainly believe what I was preaching, so I say as a man of God: The Dina plant will not close down on Wednesday, or thereafter. Furthermore, if it does close down, you can tell everybody in Tepea-pulco that the God of Terry Mize is a liar, and I'll pack my bags and leave.

"But I am here for a two-week campaign, and I am not going to pack my bags. We are going to *have* a two-week campaign!"

On the first two nights of the meeting, the people were pretty quiet. Although I preached, and God confirmed His Word, everyone was watching and waiting. Wednesday morning came around. The plant did not close. Then we had ourselves a meeting!

God moved by His Spirit in that place and showed those people the power of God. Six children, who were deaf-mutes, were completely healed by God's power. Then someone brought in a little nine-year-old girl with epilepsy.

I said, "Bring her to me tomorrow, where I am staying. I want to pray for her while her mother is there."

The mother brought the little girl, and as they walked in, she began to have an attack. I instructed the mother about what we were going to do — cast the devil out. It is important for you to understand that our conversation was in Spanish.

I said to the little girl, "Honey, say, 'I am free.'"

She (a demon in her) said, "I am Christ."

I repeated, "Say, 'I am free.'"

She said again, "I am Christ."

I said, "Say this: 'Satan, you cannot live in me.'"

She said, "Satan, I cannot live without thee."

These two phrases are similar in Spanish so I had her say it again, "Satan, you cannot live in me."

She said, "Satan, I cannot live without thee."

I told that devil I was not amused. Then I cast him out in the name of Jesus, and he left. The little girl was completely delivered by the power of God! I talked to her uncle long after that, and she still was free.

Open-air campaigns are exciting. It is necessary to have miracle-salvation meetings because you are dealing mostly with sinners. However, I love to go into the area churches and teach the faith message: that you can have what you say, and that you are the righteousness of God through Christ Jesus. The people get excited when they hear this.

The Faith Message Is Exciting
• • •

In one particular meeting a lady with a large growth on her stomach came forward. When I prayed for her, that thing disappeared. About three months later, I saw her pastor. He said that after I left, the growth came back, and her children rushed her to Mexico City. The doctors said the growth had to be removed immediately, so they started to prepare for her surgery.

The lady thought, "What in the world am I doing here? When Brother Terry prayed for me, the growth left. He taught us that we are kings and priests, that we are redeemed from the curse, that we are the righteousness of God, and that Satan has no right to put anything on our bodies!"

Then she said, "Wait just a minute," went to the restroom, laid hands on that growth, and cursed it.

She said, "I do not have to put up with this; I am healed by the stripes of Jesus."

When she went back into the doctor's office and was examined, the growth was gone! They sent her home!

After another service, one lady told me this: "Last night I went over to my sister's house to visit her, her husband, and their little daughter who had been sick. While I was there, the girl went into convulsions, fell on the floor, and died! My sister and her husband became hysterical, so I screamed at them to shut up!

"I told them what I had just learned in the service — we have authority in the name of Jesus and can pray for the sick and raise the dead. I told them Jesus is greater than the devil because the Bible says, **Greater is he that is in you, than he that is in the world** (1 John 4:4). I told them we were going to pray right then and raise her up! And we did!"

It was so exciting to me that she did not come and get me to do it. When people really receive the Word that is preached, when they realize they can do signs and wonders by the power of God dwelling in them, I feel I have done my job.

After I had finished preaching one night in Guadalajara, a man came up in the prayer line. He was totally blind in one eye, and with the other eye could only distinguish light from dark in the bright sun. When I laid my hands on him, God restored his sight. Though he had not worked for eight years, he went back to work the next day.

While I was visiting him the next week, God told me that something was wrong with someone else in his family. I asked him about that. He said God had healed one of his daughters who had been hemorrhaging.

However, as I started to leave, God spoke to me again, so I turned to the man and said, "Is one of your kids sick?"

He said, "No."

But when I told him what God had just said to me, he said, "I *do* have a four-year-old grandson who has never spoken a word."

I said, "That's what God wants me to do. Bring him here."

They brought in a cute little guy named Ricardo. I rebuked the mute spirit, commanded healing to come into him, and the string on his tongue to be loosed. Then I pointed over to his mother and asked him what her name was.

He said, "Maria," and he has been talking ever since! He was healed by the power of God!

Many people tell me it is easier to see miracles in foreign fields where faith is simple. To some extent, this is true. I have also found that much of the difference lies in the minister's confession.

MIRACLES CAN HAPPEN ANYWHERE
· · ·

I used to say, "I have miracles in Mexico, but I do not have them in the United States."

Since I started confessing, "I have miracles wherever I go, because I preach the Word of God, and God confirms

His Word," I have had miracles in the United States. When you are preaching the Word of God, it is easy to have miracles anywhere.

Once, in Mexico, they brought a twenty-one-year-old boy to me who looked like a zombie. Pepe was slobbering, his pupils were dilated, and he could not walk, talk, or eat. If you lifted his arm, it would stay that way for hours. He would stay in any position in which you put him. They said he had been that way for eight days. He went to work one morning and came back in a taxi like that.

I asked the mother, "Why did you bring him here?"

She said, "Somebody told me that you could help him."

I dispatched the devil, in the name of Jesus, and got the boy to where he could talk. I sent him home, and told his family I would be over later to see him.

Several days in a row, I visited him and prayed for him. He became completely normal. I found that he had been delving into mind control which resulted in Satan controlling his mind. People are looking for reality, and to fool them, Satan has counterfeited nearly every operation of God.

In Joshua 1:8, God told Joshua to meditate in the Word. Satan counterfeits God's law because he knows that God's law works. Satan knows that meditation works. That is why he initiated transcendental meditation and yoga. The counterfeit will work up to a point — then it will kill you as it nearly did Pepe.

I went to see Pepe one evening and as I was visiting him, I felt a warning in my spirit.

I said to his mother, "When we leave tonight and he begins to vomit, do not be afraid. I feel in my spirit to tell you that. It will be all right. Pepe is delivered."

She said, "Fine. Everything is all right."

I left, but I was troubled in my spirit. The next day, I went back over to Pepe's home. He was nowhere to be seen. His mother said that he was in a mental institution!

She said, "Last night, after you left, he began to vomit this black stuff. He said that he was all right — just as you said — but I got scared and called the doctor."

After the doctor heard the story of how Pepe had come home from work like a zombie and hearing voices that said they were going to kill him, he sent him to the mental institution. (I am not against doctors. They are fighting the same things we are, but they are treating symptoms. We are trying to fight the cause.)

I said to his mother, "For eight days he was nearly dead. You did not call a doctor or take him to a hospital. You brought him to me. Now that he's all right, you call a doctor, who puts him a mental institution. Come on, we are going to see him."

"We cannot see him," she said.

I put her in my car and brought a friend of mine along. It was dark when we got to the mental institution, and it did not look inviting. I drove through the iron gates and up to the foreboding-looking building. I took my Bible, and we went inside.

My friend said, "Don't take your Bible with you; they will lock us up."

I said, "I wouldn't dream of going into that place *without* my Bible."

To the girl at the desk I said, "This is Pepe's mother. We want to see him."

The girl said, "That is prohibited." (I heard that word *prohibited* many times that night!)

"Maybe you did not understand what I said," I answered, "This is Pepe's mother. We want to see him."

She repeated, "That is prohibited."

I said, "Ma'am, I am this boy's minister. I am a missionary. I preach the Word of God to your people, and I want to see him *now*!"

Again, she said, "That is prohibited."

I had every opportunity to fail and go home. We have many such opportunities, but we have to hang on to the Word of God and push through to victory.

I slammed my Bible on her desk, beat on it, and said, "I want to see that boy, and I want to see him *now!* "

She said, "That is prohibited."

She was acting a little more cautious by then. (She thought I belonged in that place!)

I said, "I want to see somebody with more authority than you, because I am not leaving this place until I see Pepe."

Finally, she said, "All right. There is a hallway out here, and all the patients have gone to get their medications. When they come back, you can see him through the window."

"Oh, no! I am not going to see him through the window. You are going to open the door and let me go in."

I kept saying that until she finally opened the door. After telling my friend to hold the door open so she could not lock me in, I went through it and into the narrow hallway.

About one hundred and fifty patients began to walk towards me. Every demon in that place knew who I was and why I was there. My knees almost started knocking, but I refused to let them. I held my Bible in my folded arms as I kept saying, **Greater is He Who is in me than he who is in the world!**

Some of those guys came up to me and put their noses to my nose. I would say, "I rebuke you, Satan, in the name of Jesus." The patient would leave, then the next one would do the same thing, and again I stood in the authority of the name of Jesus.

Finally, Pepe came. I grabbed him, shoved him through the door, and said to my friend, "Put him in the car. We're getting out of here!"

The girl sounded the alarm, but only one guard came down. (Thank God!) She told him what I had done.

Instead of giving him time to think, I started to rebuke him. I told him that I was a man of God, that Pepe was one of my converts and would die if he stayed in the institution.

I kept telling him, "Figure up his bill, and I will pay it, if you want it paid. I am taking Pepe out of here . . . in the name of Jesus."

Finally, he said to the girl, "Figure up his bill."

He was holding a big file folder, and I said, "I want to know what kind of medicine you have been giving him."

He said, "Giving out that information is prohibited."

I snatched the file from his hand and made him write down what they had been giving Pepe as I read it off. I took the paper, paid the bill, and left!

My friend and I prayed for Pepe as we drove. By the time we reached his home, he was totally delivered! The next day, I showed the prescription to two Spirit-filled doctor friends in Guadalajara. They said the drug was institutional, the dosage was three times what anybody should ever have, and it would take three or four days for Pepe to recover. I told them that he already had recovered. I just wanted to know what the doctors had given him.

You have opportunities to do something in this world, even if it means kidnapping people from mental institutions or being shot at! The Word of God still works!

BE AN OVERCOMER
• • •

Our job is to share the Gospel with as many people as possible around the world. Jesus said that when we have done that, the end will come.

David said, **I have been young, and now am old; yet have I not seen the righteous forsaken, nor his seed begging bread** (Psalms 37:25).

If you have ever had the desire to go to the mission fields, I can share with you the things that will work in your everyday life to put you over. God will put you over by making you a conqueror — even **more than a conqueror** (Romans 8:37). God's Word will let you whip the devil, hands down. It will put food on your table and clothes on your back. It is nice to hear that in church, but

I am a living example that God's Word works in everyday life.

Once, when I was about seventeen years old, I had been preaching in my home church where I was a youth director. I stayed until everybody left, then I locked up and walked out. Just as I put my hand on the car door, somebody grabbed me, shoved me against the car, and put a switchblade knife to my throat.

"I am going to kill you," he said.

The first thing that came out of my mouth was, "Devil, take your hands off God's anointed, in the name of Jesus!"

Looking at me kind of funny, he took the knife away from my throat, turned around, and ran off. These things will work for you as well as me! Take God's Word into both ears, inject it into your heart, then let it come out your spirit and out your mouth.

C H A P T E R 8

An Angel Before Thee
. . .

**Behold, I send an Angel before thee, to
keep thee in the way, and to bring thee into
the place which I have prepared.**

Exodus 23:20

The pastor in a little Baptist mission in Oaxaca, Mexico, was preaching the Word of God and making the unbelievers angry, so some of them decided to kill him. While he was preaching one night, they surrounded the church. There was only one way out, so a mob waited for him there with machetes, sticks, and stones.

When the preacher finished his sermon, and all the believers had gone home, he said, "Well, God, I have to go out there. I don't mind going to heaven. If it's my time to go, I'll go. But I don't think You are through with me yet. So I'm going out there and believe You. Whatever You decide is all right with me."

When he walked out of the church, that angry mob just backed up and gave him plenty of room. He walked right through the crowd, went home, and fell asleep.

The next day, a man came to him and said, "We thought you were alone in church."

"I was," he said.

"Oh, no, you weren't," the man exclaimed.

"Yes, I was. There wasn't anybody in there but me."

"No," the man insisted, "when you walked out, there were two big guys with you. They were wearing cowboy hats and had guns on their hips."

God has a sense of humor! He sent His Texas angels!

GOD'S ARMY IN WHITE
• • •

In Ixmiquilpan, Mexico, the Otomi Indians have one of the largest Protestant churches in Latin America. On Pentecost Sunday or Easter, they will have as many as eight or nine thousand people crammed into the church, standing shoulder to shoulder.

When the church started in the 1940's, the pastor preached the Gospel and made the people furious. Some Christians there were martyred. Unbelievers would drag them through the cactus patches until their faces were literally scraped off, then they would shoot them.

The persecution became so bad that the believers moved up to a little barren hill and lived there. They named it "Mount Calvary."

God continued to work through them, and they kept getting more and more converts. Finally, the unbelievers in the valley below decided they were going to wipe them out. Instead of killing them one by one, they were going to kill them all. That night the unbelievers surrounded the hill and marched together up toward "Mount Calvary."

Halfway up, they ran into an army that was dressed in white and fully armed. They made a hasty retreat back down the hill! Several months later they began talking to some of the believers and wanted to know where they got their army. Of course, the believers did not know anything about an attack, or an army, or a retreat. They were just up there praying — and God sent His army to stop the attack!

Needless to say, that is why the church is there and why it is so large. I have preached there many times, and each campaign has witnessed that God confirms His Word. There were many miracles as He confirmed His Word to the Otomi Indians. The day is not over when God is doing supernatural things. He is indeed confirming His Word and doing the supernatural today.

GOD STILL HAS HIS RECIPE FOR MANNA
• • •

When I read about the children of Israel walking around in the desert, I get happy. Their clothes never wore out. They had a cloud by day to protect them from the sun. They had a pillar of fire by night to keep them warm. They had a rock that would give them water to drink. The Bible says there was not a feeble one among them. They had daily manna! Fresh bread from heaven!

People think God does not have the recipe for manna anymore. Let me take this opportunity to tell you that He does! People around the world are dying of hunger. If they would just use their faith, God would provide manna.

Just because He shut down the bakery does not mean He took the ovens out! He still has the recipe for manna. If people can believe God, He will feed them.

When Elijah sat by the brook, the ravens brought him meat and bread. The supernatural never runs short, only the natural dries up. When you go around preaching the Gospel, God will never run short. You can depend on His Word.

Jackie and I have traveled all over Mexico with absolutely no money. We have gone places and done things without even stopping to think about it. When we did, we realized how many times God had supernaturally intervened in our lives.

When we first went to Mexico, it was simply because God said, "Go." Even though our only contact in Mexico died just before we were ready to go, we still went.

I had the address of one Mexican family, so I wrote them a letter saying, "This sister that we both know died, but my wife and I are believing God. We are coming to Mexico to minister."

The lady wrote back and told us to come. When we went, we did not even have a car. We sold everything and had nothing left, including money! (I do not advise anyone to do that unless you are positive it is God.)

Then a friend of mine from McAlester, Oklahoma, who had a Cessna 206 airplane, called me and said, "Terry, I understand that you are going to Mexico."

"That's right."

I had no idea when we were leaving; but when he asked, I said, "Next Thursday."

I did not know how we were going to get to Mexico. I just spoke it out: "We are leaving next Thursday."

Then he said, "I'll fly you down in my plane if you will pay the expenses."

"How much are the expenses?"

"About $200."

"Okay. Be here on Wednesday."

After my friend agreed to come on Wednesday, I heard myself say, "Fine, I'll have the $200."

My head was screaming at me! There was no way to get that money. Several people had called and asked if we needed anything.

I would say, "Absolutely not! My needs are met according to God's riches in glory by Christ Jesus. Thank you."

There was a reason for this: When Jackie and I went into the ministry, we said, "God, we'll not make our needs known to anybody. We'll never ask a man for a place to preach."

And we have never done that. I have never called a pastor and said, "Brother, I'm going to be in your area. Would you like me to come by and share with your congregation?"

Please understand that I am not criticizing anybody who does that. You must do it the way God leads *you*, but God did not tell me to do it that way.

I said, "God, I'm working for You. Since You are my employer, I expect You to treat me better and pay me better than a natural employer would:

"I don't ever want to be broke.

"As the cost of living goes up, I expect You to raise my salary.

"If we starve, we will starve in the name of Jesus. If we go under, it's because You went under."

As you know, God has never gone under, and we are not going under! He has continued to support us and protect us. That is how we went into the ministry, and we are still operating the same way.

The only mission board I have ever had is the Father, the Son, and the Holy Ghost! I work for GOD, SON & COMPANY, and they pay very well!

The night before my friend was to fly us to Mexico, we went over to visit with my family. As we were driving away, God told me to go by and see some other people.

Frankly, I did not want to, so I did not. I just kept on driving toward home.

In just a little bit, Jackie said, "I think God just told me to go see so-and-so."

I said, "I know it. He told me, too; but I don't want to go over there. I want to go home."

She said, "Well, if God told both you and me, I guess we had better go see them."

So we drove to their house. When the lady came to the door and saw us, she began to jump up and down and praise God!

The Lord had told her that day to give us $250. She had worried all day about how to tell her husband, but God told him the same thing while he was on the job. They did not know how to contact us, and then we appeared at their door!

I paid my friend $200 to fly us into Oaxaca, Mexico. That is not the end of the world, but it certainly is visible from there!

As that plane flew off into the sunset, we started our missionary career with $50 in our pocket and no church or other means of support. But we had the Word of God!

There have been times when God has said to me, "My Word is better than money in your pocket."

GOD DOES NOT LIVE IN A MAILBOX
. . .

Many times, God gives us a word, and we make an entire sentence out of it. God spoke to us in Oaxaca and told us to go to Guadalajara.

I said, "All right, I'll go."

I really thought I would go there to study the language. I found out later that God wanted us to live there and start a work.

When God spoke to me about going to Guadalajara, I asked, "When do You want us to go?"

"This week," He said.

There was Jackie, myself, and our two-year-old son, plus a 27-year-old girl who had come with us to Mexico. She wanted to see what it was like on the mission field. There were four of us, and I had no money. So I did what all good missionaries do — I religiously went to the mailbox.

At the time we believed, just like all missionaries do, that God lived in a mailbox! We believed that as God spoke to people in the United States, they would send us money in the mail. God has since shown us that He does not live in a mailbox. He can supply our needs in the country or out of it. He has met our needs even when I did not have a post office box.

GOD KNOWS YOUR ADDRESS
. . .

How is it that God could find Moses, wandering out there in the desert? He did not have an address or a post office box. Yet, God found him.

God found Elijah sitting by a brook.

He found the children of Israel when they were in the desert.

Some people think God has lost their addresses, but always God knows where you are. To keep in touch with Him, you must do something first: Start releasing your faith instead of your needs. God will meet your faith.

I religiously went to the mailbox, but nothing was there.

When God told me to go to Guadalajara, it was Tuesday, so I said, "If You want me to go this week, I'll go Friday." (I gave myself as much time as possible to get some money.)

In Mexico, all roads lead to Mexico City. To get to Guadalajara, I had to go by bus first to Mexico City, which was two hundred and sixty miles. In a plane, it only takes forty-five minutes, but by bus it takes thirteen hours. I had money to buy bus tickets to Mexico City, with $8 left over.

I continued going to the mailbox — nothing! Friday came — nothing! Faith demands action, so we packed our bags and did all we could do. Then, I did something that I *do not* do anymore: I got under the circumstances.

I told Jackie, "All I know to do is exercise my faith. I'll go to town and buy our bus tickets to Mexico City. Then God will have to do a miracle. We will have only $8 left over, and we can't get from Mexico City to Guadalajara on $8 — not by a burro, or bus, or any other way."

In the place where we lived, to go to town, you had to walk up a hill and through a cornfield for a mile to reach the city busline. As I dragged myself through that hot cornfield, I had my own pity party.

The buses in Mexico carry turkeys, chickens, and goats, as well as people. I have ridden many a mile with pigs and hogs on the floor of the bus. It has been so bad at times that I have ridden on the bumper of the bus, hanging on to the rain gutter with my fingers, just so I could be outside. I did not do that because I was poor, but because it is the only transportation. In those countries, you can have the very best in town and still not have very much.

I slumped onto the front seat of the bus, with my arms crossed and my head hanging down, feeling sorry for myself. Then God spoke to me, and I answered Him out loud. I do not know what the other people thought as I sat there on the front seat talking to empty space.

God said, "Don't you know that Jesus has access to anything to which I have access to? Don't you know that anything I have, He can get any time He wants it?"

"Yes, Sir."

"Don't you know that you are an heir and a joint-heir with Him?"

"Yes, Sir."

"Then act like it. If you needed money, would your natural father give it to you?"

"Yes, Sir."

"If you were really in a bind and needed it, would a friend give it to you?"

"Probably."

"Don't you think that I am better than they?"

God had crashed my pity party!

I sat up straight in my seat, as I rode the rest of the way. I went into the bus station, got in line, took out my money, and bought our tickets to Mexico City. I put the $8 change into my pocket and went home.

When I walked back through that cornfield, I was walking on a cloud. I did not have any money and I did not have tickets to Guadalajara. But I did not need money. I had God's Word! God would provide for our getting to Guadalajara. My God confirms His Word!

When I got home, I was so excited and radiant that Jackie thought I had been to the mailbox and received some money from the States.

I said, "No, I have something better than money. I have the Word of God! God says we have it, and I'm not going to argue with Him."

When we boarded the bus it was about 9 p.m. We erroneously thought that we would be able to get some sleep. According to one guidebook, within one hour's time on that road, there are eleven hundred curves. I believe it!

We got into Mexico City about 8 a.m. without getting any sleep on the way.

Jackie said, "Well, here we are in Mexico City. What are we going to do with only $8 in our pockets?"

"All I know to do is take a taxi to the other bus station and stand in line for our other tickets."

Jackie, who was expecting our son, said, "I'm so tired. It was a thirteen-hour bus ride with diesel fumes blowing in the windows when we rounded the curves. Can't we go to Wayne and Martha Myers' house and rest just a little while?"

We had just met Wayne and Martha and barely knew them, but they had told us to come by and spend the night with them on the way to Guadalajara. I had determined not to do that, and neither Jackie nor I had said anything about our needs.

But I said, "Well, let's go by their house. You can rest for a little while — then we're leaving."

When we got to the Myers' house, Jackie went straight to bed.

In a few minutes Wayne came in and said, "You are going to spend the night, aren't you?"

"No."

"Well, what are you going to do?"

"We are taking the bus to Guadalajara," I said.

"We are going to Guadalajara this week, but we're going by train. You ought to do that instead of taking the bus. It is a Pullman. You can have your own sleeping car, and you won't be cramped as you are on the bus. In the

91

train, you can go up to the dining car. Everything is nice. You ought to do that."

"Well, praise God, I believe I will," I said, as I sat there with only $8 in my pocket.

Then Wayne said, "I'm going to get my tickets now. Why don't you pick up yours, too?"

I said, "All right, I will."

As I walked out to Wayne's car, my head was screaming at me, and the devil was screaming at me, but my spirit was saying, "My needs are met according to His riches in glory by Christ Jesus."

While we were driving across Mexico City, getting closer and closer to the train station, my mind yelled louder and louder.

Wayne said, "You know, it's going to be a miracle if you get those tickets."

I thought, "Brother, it will be a bigger miracle than you think!"

Wayne explained, "I had to order my tickets weeks in advance. You want yours just a few hours in advance, so it's going to be a miracle!"

"That's all right. God specializes in miracles. We'll get them."

Wayne did not know that I had no money for tickets. I did not tell them what really happened that night until two or three years later.

As we pulled into the parking lot, Wayne said, "God just told me to give you a hundred dollars."

I said, "Well, praise God!"

As we walked into the station house, I was thinking, "I've still got to pay for the tickets. He hasn't given me the money yet."

Wayne, who speaks fluent Spanish, walked up to the window and said, "I'll order the tickets."

He ordered the tickets, and I reached into my pocket.

Then he said, "I'll pay for them. You can pay me back in just a little bit."

I said, "All right."

He was excited because we were able to get the tickets so soon, but I was *more* excited! We drove back to the house; and, when we went inside, Wayne said to Martha, "God told me not only to give these kids a hundred dollars, but to buy their train tickets."

Wayne gave us the train tickets, the $100, *and* took us to the train station. When we got to Guadalajara, we had $108 in our pockets! The Word of God works!

We knew nobody in town, and we had no place to stay. That $108 was eaten up quickly by hotel bills. And I had no mailbox in Guadalajara! Nevertheless, God miraculously supplied us with a house and food. It was beautiful and exciting!

GOD WORKS IN THE SUPERNATURAL
• • •

If you take the miracles out of the Bible, there will not be much left.

If you take the miracles out of the church today, you will not have much left.

93

**Behold, I send an Angel before thee, to
keep thee in the way, and to bring thee into
the place which I have prepared.**

Exodus 23:20

God confirms His Word with signs and miracles.

Once when I was praying, I said, "God, why is it that
when I share these things that are so real to me and to my
family, they do not seem as real to the people to whom I
am ministering?"

The answer God gave me was this: "It is real to you
because you have to use My Word on a daily basis or you
will go under."

If I do not use my faith, I do not eat — and I like to
eat! There is no paycheck coming in, and if I do not use
my faith, my kids do not eat.

If I do not use my faith, we cannot pay our rent.

If I do not use my faith, we will not have a car to drive,
or gasoline to put in the car. That is why it is so real to us!

The term "living by faith" is so abused. Many times
when you tell somebody you are living by faith, they will
say, "Oh, I'm so sorry." To them it conveys or denotes
poverty. All I can say is this: Living by faith is the greatest
thing I have ever done.

I love the Word of God. I have no higher ambition
than to be a missionary. I have no higher ambition for my
children than to see them preaching the Gospel around
this world, giving Living Bread to dying men. You know,
many times we have our children's lives so planned out
that we know what college we want them to attend, what
they will do after college, and who they will marry. We

need to release our kids and let God do something with
them!

Three Concepts People Live By

There are three concepts by which people can live. Jesus illustrated these in the story of the Good Samaritan. You have probably known it since you were a child.

> A certain man went down from Jerusalem to Jericho, and fell among thieves, which stripped him of his raiment, and wounded him, and departed, leaving him half dead.
>
> And by chance there came down a certain priest that way: and when he saw him, he passed by on the other side.
>
> And likewise a Levite, when he was at the place, came and looked on him, and passed by on the other side.
>
> But a certain Samaritan, as he journeyed, came where he was: and when he saw him, he had compassion on him,
>
> And went to him, and bound up his wounds, pouring in oil and wine, and set him on his own beast, and brought him to an inn, and took care of him.
>
> And on the morrow when he departed, he took out two pence, and gave them to the

host, and said unto him, Take care of him; and
whatsoever thou spendest more, when I come
again, I will repay thee.

Which now of these three, thinkest thou,
was neighbour unto him that fell among the
thieves?

Luke 10:30-36

Concept #1: Whatever is thine is mine, and I will take
it from you if I can.

When this man went down to Jericho, thieves
attacked him. They stripped him of his clothing, wounded
him, and left him naked and almost dead. They took
everything he had and left him lying there.

Their concept, or philosophy of life, was: "Whatever
belongs to you belongs to me, and I'll get it any way I possibly can."

That's the way the world's system operates.

Concept #2: What's mine is mine.

Jesus then said that two religious men came by. These
men obviously were not spiritual, just religious. One was
a priest; the other was a Levite. They came along at different times, but both of them looked over and saw the man
lying there. In those days everyone carried his own first-
aid kit — with oil, wine, and bandages — because they all
walked long distances.

Perhaps the two religious men thought the thieves
who had robbed and hurt the man could still be lurking
around, and if they stopped to help him, the thieves could
come out of hiding and do the same thing to them. Whatever their thoughts were, they decided to keep their goods

to themselves. They walked to the other side of the road and went on their way.

Their concept, or philosophy of life, was: "What is mine is mine, and I will keep it if I can. What belongs to me is mine, so keep your hands off it!"

Many Christians live that way today.

Concept #3: What's mine is thine, and you can have it if you need it.

Later, a Samaritan passed by. Jesus used a Samaritan for an example because he was not someone acceptable. Jews hated Samaritans as "half-breeds." They called them "mongrels." The situation was sort of like whites and blacks after the Civil War. The Samaritan was not of Israel and was an outsider, which is why Jesus chose to use him as a drastic example of who one's neighbor really is. Here was this man showing compassion to a person of a race who despised him.

Jesus said that when the Samaritan came along and saw the man lying there, he immediately went over and took care of him. If you picture the Samaritan in our modern-day setting, he would have put the wounded man in his car, or hailed a taxicab, and taken the man to the local motel or hospital.

He would have whipped out his credit card and said, "Here, just put it on my bill. Whatever the man needs, let him sign the ticket. I'll take care of it. No matter what he spends or what he does, I'll pay for it."

The Good Samaritan did not know the wounded man, but his concept, or philosophy of life, was: "What I have is yours. You can have it if you need it or want it."

That was the example Jesus chose to give — loving those who despise you. Most Christians do not live by the concept of the thieves: "Whatever is yours is mine, and I'll take it from you if I can." However, it seems that many have the same attitude as the two religious men: "Whatever is mine is mine." And they have the feeling certain people are to be shunned. A derelict by the side of the road might contaminate the "Christian."

They are not like the thieves, who actually take things from people by force, but they do sit on their own possessions and say, "Keep your hands off! That belongs to me." And they do hold themselves aloof from certain classes of the needy.

Jesus wants us to be like the Samaritan. He wants us to live and walk in the nature of God — to look for a place to give, a place where we can help. Love compels us to give. **God so loved the world, that he gave his only begotten Son** (John 3:16). He so loved the world that He *gave* with no respecting of persons. Love compels us to share.

God says, "What is Mine is thine, and you can have it if you want it or because you need it."

That is how we ought to live with God and with our fellow man.

We should say to God: "Whatever I have, You have provided it for me in the first place. It belongs to You, so anytime You need it or want it, just let me know. I am only a steward over it, just taking care of it."

A steward is someone who takes care of another person's money or property. We need to be good stewards over what God gives us. God is a good God. Our Father wants us to have things, but it is wrong for things to have us. We can have diamond rings, fur coats, new homes, fishing and hunting equipment, airplanes, or anything as long as they do not have us.

We must always realize that we are not the owner of our things but the steward of them. When God says, "Let it go," we need to let go.

From Giving To Live to Living To Give
• • •

Having been raised a Christian, I knew what the Word of God said about giving and tithing. I have always been a faithful tither. Whenever I got any money, one-tenth of it always went in the offering because it belonged to God.

It was different for Jackie. Because she went to church only on Christmas and Easter, she did not have a lot of doctrine to "unlearn" as many people do. Some people go to church all their lives, then get filled with the Holy Spirit and have to unlearn all the "religion" they have learned.

I believe that is why Jackie caught on to the faith message so easily. She believed what the Word of God said without filtering it through doctrines and traditions. Before Jackie learned about tithing and giving to the Lord, she would make me empty my pockets before we went to a meeting.

She would then hand me two or three dollars to give in the offering as she said, "You'll go down there and give everything we've got!"

I knew that the Word of God worked, so I showed it to Jackie in the Bible. Once she saw it and accepted it, she said, "Yeah, I see that!"

So we started giving. We realized that we could give to God and get our needs met. One of the greatest books I have ever read is *Miracle of Seed-Faith*[1] by Oral Roberts. It excited me because it went along with the Word of God.

We started planting seeds, and planting more seeds! (Oral Roberts made that term famous!) We realized that we could give in order to live. If you have a need staring you in the face — an unpaid bill or a problem — you can give to God, or plant a seed into the harvest, and it will grow. Then you will get more than you gave. The law of the harvest is a spiritual law of God. That is why it works in all areas, from planting a garden to planting for finances.

A farmer plants corn in the ground, knowing that more corn will be harvested than was planted. If he planted only one kernel and reaped only one kernel, he would be wasting his time. He knows he is going to get back more that he planted because that is a natural law. However, the natural law works because it is based on a spiritual law.

When Jackie and I had a need, we would give; and God would bless us. We would pay off the need, and we would live. We were giving to live.

LIVING TO GIVE
• • •

Then, after we met Wayne and Martha Myers, we shifted gears and moved up into a new realm. We moved

---

[1]Roberts, Oral. *Miracle of Seed-Faith* (Tulsa: Oral Roberts, 1970).

out of *giving to live* and moved up to the realm of *living to give*. Wayne and Martha have been such a blessing to us. This message on living to give, as well as many other things in this book, I learned from them.

Living to give means: Looking for an opportunity to place finances, to invest, in the Gospel. Some years ago, I saw Wayne stand up and promise to give $10,000 to a certain organization. He paid it off in one year's time — and he is a faith missionary! He lives by faith, not by a fixed income of support.

The next year, he stood up and said, "I'll give $25,000."

They gave him two years to pay it off, but he paid off his pledge in one year!

The third year, he stood and said, "I'll give $100,000."

Can you imagine a faith missionary who lives in Mexico giving $100,000? All he has to depend on is God!

When we got to know Wayne and Martha Myers, we saw two people living to give. They look for places to invest in the Gospel. They look for opportunities to get involved in the Gospel around the world.

Once, Jackie and I were sitting on the platform as Wayne was ministering at Christ For the Nations Institute in Dallas, Texas.

Wayne said, "One of these men on the platform needs a car."

That afternoon, I went to Wayne and said, "The guy who needs a car is Brother so-and-so, right?"

Wayne said, "It has been taken care of. Don't concern yourself with it."

"What did you do — give him *your* car?"

"Yes," he said.

Wayne is living to give! Though he had things to do and places to go, he gave away the only vehicle he had. It had been given to him; then he gave it away.

Jackie and I have given away cars. When we started operating in this principle, I will never forget how it made people mad. The same thing happens when you make a quality decision not to be sick anymore: All of your church "friends" get angry at you.

One pastor said, "Terry believes you can say, 'Gimmie, gimmie, gimmie,' and God will give you a Cadillac! It doesn't work that way."

But the next time I came to town I was driving a Cadillac! Someone had given it to me! Then we gave it away, and people could not believe it. They asked me why I did not sell the car and use the money to go to the mission fields.

I said, "I don't live by the law of buying and selling. I live by the law of giving and receiving. If I sell a Cadillac, I can get a few thousand dollars; but, if I give it away, I get a hundredfold in return!"

People like to make money, and the best way I know of to do that is to give to the Gospel.

In 2 Corinthians 4:18 Paul said:

> While we look not at the things which are
> seen, but at the things which are not seen: for
> the things which are seen are temporal; but
> the things which are not seen are eternal.

That sounds like double-talk, but it is not. Let me break it down into modern English and see what Paul really said:

"Don't look at the things which you can see with your physical eyes, because those things are temporary. They will not last. They will decay and pass away."

GOD'S WORD IS ETERNAL
• • •

The chair in your house will not last; it is temporary. The clothes on your body will not last; they will rot away. The car that you are driving may be brand new, and you may have paid $20,000 for it; but look at it in two years. It will start decaying, especially if you live on the Gulf Coast. In Houston and Corpus Christi, Texas, people own brand-new cars that have already started to erode.

These things are temporary. They will not last. They will pass away. Your body will not last; it will die — unless Jesus comes first. Everything you can see, taste, touch, smell, or hear is temporary.

All of our lives we have been taught that the five physical senses are reality. No! The Word of God is reality. You will find that the five physical senses, and the Word of God do not agree during the first round. Whenever I start to do anything for God, I always have a battle: On one side are the five physical senses and on the other side is the Word of God.

The two sides never agree. Some things in the Word do not sound right, smell right, feel right, look right, or taste right. Yet the Word of God says they *are* right. I have found that when I go with the Word of God, my senses change. All of a sudden, what the Word says looks, smells, feels, sounds and tastes right.

If you do it the way Grandma says, or tradition says, or the way it is done at "the First Church," it never works. The five physical senses are not reality. The natural "reality" is temporary and will pass away.

The Word of God is reality. We need to operate according to it instead of according to how something feels, looks, tastes, smells, or sounds.

Paul was saying, "Look at the things that you cannot see with your physical eye, because those things are eternal. Only what you do for God will last."

I want you to realize that anything you have in this world will not last and amounts to garbage. If it does not relate to eternity, it is garbage. Again, I am not saying that you must live in poverty. I do not believe that, and I do not live that way. I preach the prosperity message in places where people tell me it will not work. I preach it in Mexico, in Honduras, and in Guatemala, and I see people prospering when it is impossible in the natural for them to do so. They prosper because they receive the Word of God.

Some missionaries were giving me trouble once, because I was preaching the prosperity message.

They said, "Do not preach that, Brother Terry. It does not work down here. These people do not know they are poor until you tell them. They do not know there is a better way until you tell them. You just make them miserable because there is no way they can have prosperity."

The missionaries kept saying, "It will not work. It will not work!"

But I kept preaching this:

"In Luke 6:38, Jesus said: **Give, and it shall be given unto you; good measure, pressed down, and shaken together, and running over, shall men give into your bosom.** God will bless you. What you give for the Gospel's sake will be returned to you and much more, both in this life and in the one to come.

"God is your shepherd; you do not have to lack or want for anything. He will meet all your needs according to His riches in glory by Christ Jesus. Whatever you desire, you can have."

A FAMILY WHO ACTED ON HIS WORD
. . .

When we were living in Guadalajara, a family invited me to hold prayer meetings in their home two nights a week. Every Tuesday and Thursday, I went to their tiny house. It had one big room. There were dirt walls and a table in the middle of the room, which they carried outside in order to gain space. Seventy people jam-packed that little mud hut! It was wall-to-wall people!

My back was shoved against the wall, and my Bible was held tightly against my chest. In those tight quarters, I preached the Word, and God moved there in the suburbs of Guadalajara: the blind saw, the deaf heard, miracles were performed.

The family who invited me into their home was poor, but they invited me to eat with them.

I said, "No. I would rather eat at home with my family."

But they persisted, "No, we will not hear of that. Every Tuesday and Thursday, you are eating with us."

So, every Tuesday and Thursday, when I had finished preaching and the people had gone home, they carried the table back into the room, and the lady cooked supper. When we sat down to eat, it was usually around midnight.

Mexico is the only place in the world where you eat your spoon when you have finished your meal. It takes skill to eat a fried egg with a tortilla! When I first started, bean juice ran down my elbow. Now I can eat beans and eggs on a tortilla with the best of them!

Paul said that he came in demonstration of the Holy Spirit and power. (1 Corinthians 2:1-4). I have always believed that.

When you are dealing with thousands of people in a campaign, there has to be a demonstration of the Holy Ghost on the first night of the meeting, or the people will not come back on the second night. They want to see miracles; God has to do something — and He does!

One night, I brought several people with me to the prayer meeting. They wanted to see the power of God and the demonstration of the Holy Ghost. After the service as we were eating, the lady of the house broke down and started sobbing. We just sat there and waited for her to tell us her problem.

Finally she regained her composure and said, "Brother Terry, for five years we have not had enough food to feed us all. I have watched my kids go to bed hungry. It broke my heart as a mother. For five years my husband has had only one pair of pants. I have sewn those pants until all that was holding them together was the new thread.

"But since you have been coming to our house and teaching us the Word of God, things have changed. You have been telling us to give. Even when we did not have anything to give, we would give a smile, then just a centavo, then a peso, then something else. We just started giving.

"Since that day, my kids have not gone to bed hungry — not one time! I feed them consistently — on a regular basis. Besides that, I feed you every Tuesday and Thursday, as well as anyone you bring with you, and we can send out for Cokes (a luxury in Mexico).

"My husband now has five pairs of new pants, and they have elevated him at his job to a position of authority!"

Those people started giving, and that was the way God could bless them. He could not get finances into their hands until they released or planted the seed first. I cried all the way home that night.

I yelled out, "God, it works! It works! It works even in Mexico!"

I could forget about the criticism I had received from those other missionaries who said the "principle of sowing seeds" did not work everywhere. Thank God, it does work! If it does not work in Mexico, it will not work anywhere.

Giving works. Every now and then, I will walk through my house, look around, and say, "Could I give that? Could I get rid of that? Is there anything there I could not get rid of without it pricking my heart?"

If there is anything there that pricks a little, it is gone on short notice! I refuse to have anything that stands between me and God. I refuse to have anything that is closer to my heart than God. God does not care if you have any of those things. Just make sure they do not have you. Keep a sign that says "Give Away" in the glove compartment of your car!

I moved from the realm of giving to live into the realm of living to give, and I am glad!

Using Your Faith

* * *

A little boy came up to me in one service and said, "Brother Terry, I think it would hurt my heart to give away my minibike, so I need to give it to the ministry.

I sat down, talked to him, and told him he did not have to do that. Being willing to give his bike away if God asked him to was enough.

Another time I was in a church that needed to raise $22,000 for a building, when a lady came up to me after the service and said, "I want to give $5,000."

I said, "I do not want to play on your emotions. I did not come here to make you feel guilty that you live in America, own two cars, live in a nice house, and can do things people in other countries cannot.

"I do not want you to step out beyond your faith. If you have $100-faith, do not believe God for $1,000. If you have $1,000-faith, do not jump out there for $5,000. You have to progressively use your faith. Give what you have got with what faith you can embrace. Next year, it will be more, and after that, it will be more. You start by looking at a reasonable thing you can do."

Then the lady explained, "I know how to hear from God and how to give to God. I have done this before, and it is exciting! God blesses me! I am giving $5,000."

God forbid that I ever use any "gimmicks" to get people to give over and above their level of faith! I just want to share from God's Word the naked truth on stewardship. I want people to wake up to the fact that the world is dying without Jesus. There is a world where you live, and there is a world outside of where you live, and the people in both worlds need to hear about Jesus.

Laws To Live By
. . .

I say again: Anything we have that does not relate to eternity is garbage.

I have watched people all of my life — grabbing, fighting, kicking, scratching, and biting — trying to get hold of things that can only be used sixty or seventy years. When they finally get them, they are too worn out to enjoy them because of the way they went after them. The law of sin and death has taken control of their bodies. I am not saying you have to die at sixty or seventy; but, if you operate that way, you will. You need to operate on the Word of God.

You need to live by the law of the open hand and the open heart. Do not live by the law of the closed fist and the closed heart. God cannot put anything in a closed fist — only in an open hand. You have to give out. You have to let it flow out from you.

Do not live by the law of the rake or the hoe. They just reach out and pull it back to you. Learn to live by the law of the shovel — keep pouring it out.

I have seen Wayne Myers walk into an auditorium with a bushel of corn, a shovel, and a teaspoon. He would begin to preach on Luke 6:38:

Give, and it shall be given unto you; good measure, pressed down, and shaken together, and running over, shall men give into your bosom.

But there is a catch to this. In the latter part of the verse it says:

For with the same measure that ye mete withal it shall be measured to you again.

Everyone knows there are different means of measuring. Most ladies are familiar with the measures of teaspoons, cups, pints, and gallons.

I have seen Wayne reach into the basket with the teaspoon, pick up some corn, and say, "Here You are, Lord. Here is Your measure."

He would then point out how when the time comes for our measure, or our time of need, we say, "Oh, God, I have to have a miracle! I've got to have some finances."

God says, "Certainly, child. Lend Me your teaspoon."

We say, "Oh, Lord, a teaspoon won't do this time. I have to have a miracle!"

God cannot violate His own law, which says: **With the same measure that ye mete withal it shall be measured to you again.** Your harvest will be a *little* bigger than the seed, but it is the same measure. When we give God a little bit that we have, He gives us a little bit that He has. If we give God all we have, He will give us all He has.

I have then heard Wayne say, "Now if we were giving to God with a shovel, when it comes time for us to get the blessing, He will reach in His basket with that shovel and pour it back upon us."

He would then ask, "How many of you want shovels full of blessings?"

If the people made the mistake of raising their hands, he would throw shovels full of corn on them, and the corn would fly all over the auditorium! People were digging corn out of their hair and their clothing, as they saw a very effective illustration.

Just Sharing It Around
· · ·

Many times, I have gone into Mexico and said, "Here, God. This is all of it."

Then I would give away all that I had the first day, and say, "Now I do not have any money, but I know I will not be broke because I'm working for You. I have given You all that I have — the measure is a hundred percent — and I expect all that You have."

Then somebody would come along that day and give me some money.

That night some missionaries would come in, and I would empty my pockets, saying, "All right, Lord, I have given all."

Then somebody would come along and hand me some more money. But whenever someone would come along with a need, I would do the same thing. That could go on every day for a week at a time! I would give away money, then somebody would come along and hand me some more money. We were just sharing it around.

However, I do not like the term, "I gave somebody some money."

I like this better: "God told me to share it with you."

If you say, "It all belongs to God, and we are His children — just sharing it around," you are on an equal plane — just living to give.

GIMMIES AND WANTS
• • •

When we first started going to conventions years ago, I would take all the money we had (which was not much in those days), and I would change it into one-dollar bills. I knew there would be plenty of opportunities to give.

Since then, we have graduated from dollar bills to bigger and better things; but we have not changed our method. We still share everything we possibly can.

In one particular service, the man who was preaching had a legitimate need, but we had given everything we had. We had no money left to give. Jackie, who was standing beside me, reached over and touched me.

She said, in tears, "I think God just told me to give my engagement ring."

At one time Jackie was very fond of diamonds. Diamonds used to have her. Now she has them. There is a difference. Also, of course, her engagement ring held a lot of sentimental value to her. It was a solitaire costing four or five hundred dollars in 1967, and it had increased in value since I bought it for her.

I said, "All right, you give it to the missionary," and she got delivered from the "wants." Now she can have anything, because nothing has her. Since that time, many diamonds have been given to her, and she in turn has given them away. She still has a return on diamonds coming to her.

Not too long ago, a lady gave me a couple of thousand dollars worth of diamonds and said, "I want these to go to your wife."

I said, "You want me to put them in the mission field?"

"No. I want you to give them to Jackie."

I said, "I can sell them and put the money into the mission fields."

"No," she repeated. "I want them to go to Jackie."

I asked her several times to make sure that both she and I understood what she wished done with them. I did not want her to say later that she gave me diamonds for the ministry, and I gave them to my wife.

It takes a special woman to give away her engagement ring, but that is what Jackie did, and it set her free! Some people give land, motor homes, and other equipment as if the things had become a curse or plague to them — and in some cases they have. Now they are living to give — looking for a place to invest in the Gospel.

RECEIVING BY FAITH
• • •

God has given us one car after another, and we have given them away. Once I saw a man who had a motorcycle I thought was the prettiest bike I had ever seen in my life!

I said, "I think I'll find a used one and buy it."

Jackie said, "Well, you are some faith man! Why don't you practice what you preach? If you want it, confess it with your mouth and believe it with your heart. Get it with your faith."

I said, "All right. I guess I'll have to do that."

So I set my faith and said, "God, I believe I receive a Yamaha 650, colored black and gold. I believe it is mine, and I believe I receive it, in the name of Jesus. Thank You."

I do not go around telling my confessions to the world. I keep them between myself, my family, and God. I do not tell others what I am believing for, because some people use that chance to convey to others what their needs are.

I would tell my little boy, "Do you see that motorcycle sitting in the garage? (There was not anything there in the natural.) It is a Yamaha 650, black and gold — the prettiest thing your ever saw! It's mine. I got it with my faith. I believed I received it when I prayed."

Three months later, a man came to me and said, "Come by my house."

I went to his house, which was two hundred and fifty miles away, and had dinner with him.

While we were eating, he said, "God has chosen me to make you a Yamaha rider."

I said, "What?"

"I just bought a motorcycle, and God told me to give it to you."

I asked, "What kind is it?"

"A Yamaha 650."

So I drove it home — two hundred and fifty miles!

GIVING BY FAITH
. . .

Several years later, I had scheduled a campaign, but did not have the money to go on it. That did not bother me. I have gone across the United States and Mexico before with no money.

However, at that particular time, I had been making statements like this: "You may have to sell something to make your word good. You may have to change your standard of living to give to missions."

God will not allow me to preach what He does not require me to live twenty-four hours of the day. When suddenly I needed $1,000 for the campaign, the money was not there.

The first thing I thought about was my motorcycle. I picked up the telephone, called the Yamaha place, and asked if they wanted to buy it. They paid me $1,000 for it, even though it was not worth that. At that time you could have bought a new one for $1,600. In fifteen minutes on a Saturday morning, I had traded my bike and the title, and was on my way to Mexico. My wife had cried about it.

She said, "But it's your motorcycle — you got it with your faith."

"That doesn't bother me. I now have a hundredfold return on motorcycles coming to me!"

You cannot stop this principle of living to give! I gave my motorcycle for the Gospel's sake, so I cannot help but receive a motorcycle.

Use your faith! It works!

CHAPTER 12

Plant a Bigger Field – Reap a Bigger Harvest
. . .

I hate to spend money on myself. I do not mind spending it on Jackie and the kids, or other people; I just do not like to spend money on me. I have believed God for all the clothes I have, and I like it that way. I set my faith and believe Him for clothes, then He supplies.

Of course, I plant clothes in the Gospel (not my old ones, but new ones). I do not want to reap old, worn-out clothes. I want to reap new ones! I spend my money on the mission fields, and God supplies me with clothes. I have bought a total of two suits in all the years we have been in the ministry. I wore one of them once, then gave it away.

One day, Jackie said, "Terry, you are an ambassador for God. You cannot keep wearing 'skuzzy-looking' brown shoes."

Finally, I said, "All right, if it's that big a deal with you and if it will make you happy, I'll set my faith and believe God for some brown shoes. Thank You, God, for some brown shoes to match my brown suit. I believe I receive them when I pray, in Jesus' name. Amen."

A few days later, I was supposed to speak in Dallas, Texas, and Charles Capps was having a meeting at the church Jerry Savelle was then pastoring in Fort Worth. On Saturday night, I attended that meeting. On Saturday afternoon, we went by a little store I had never seen before.

I said, "Lord, since I am believing You for some shoes, just make them _____ shoes," and I named a popular brand.

In the back of this store, there were some of those shoes on sale at 40 percent off! I did not want to buy the shoes because I had asked God to supply them for me; but when God gives me a good deal on something, I will tell people He gave me a good deal. I decided to go ahead and buy the shoes because of the good deal, and they did fit. I was not excited about it, however. To me, that was second best.

That night in Fort Worth, I put on my new shoes and my new brown suit and went to hear Charles Capps preach. While there, I saw a minister dressed in a brown suit, but his shoes did not look too good! After the service, I walked over to the man, pulled off my shoes that I had only worn for two hours, and said, "Here. Try these on."

He tried them on and they were a perfect fit!

I said, "They are yours," and I left there sock-footed!

When I got back to the motel, Jackie asked, "Where are your new shoes?"

"I gave them away."

That did not surprise her.

She said, "You cannot stand to have anything. You always give it away!"

I replied, "Now, I have a hundredfold return, and I still have those brown shoes that I believed God for!"

The next day, we went to Dallas. After I had finished preaching, I was going down the prayer line, laying hands on people.

When I came to one man and asked him what he wanted, he said, "I'm supposed to give you some shoes."

I said, "All right. Let me finish praying for these people."

I prayed for them, then came back to him and asked, "Well, what are we going to do?"

He said, "I'm the manager of a shoe store. If you will come down to the store, I'll give you some shoes."

When we went to his store, he brought out two pairs of the brand of shoe for which I had asked God and gave them to me: a brown pair and a gray pair! I finally got my pair of brown shoes!

God Must Have Something To Multiply
• • •

That is a simple deal, but you can do the same with cars or airplanes, or anything else. It does not matter what you have. Just do not be looking at the wrong world. Do not be grabbing with both fists. Do not live with a closed heart and closed fist. Live with an open heart and an open hand. Learn to share.

Learn to say, "What is mine is Thine, Lord. Just help Yourself to it."

In the first place, if He is asking you for something, He is wanting to bless you. That is the divine law of God. You must give first, then He has something to multiply back to you. God is in the business of addition and multiplication. Satan is in the business of subtraction and division.

According to Mark 10:30, what you give for the Gospel's sake, God gives back to you one hundredfold, *now*, in this life, with eternal life in the life to come.

Some people will say, "With persecutions, Brother Terry!"

I know it says that, but you do not have to use your faith to receive persecutions. They are an automatic "blessing"! Not necessarily from God! Once you start prospering and getting back the hundredfold return, your family and friends will bring the persecution.

Whatever you give for the Gospel's sake, God multiplies it a hundredfold and gives it back. If you give God zero, He runs it through His computer and multiplies it one hundred times back to you, but you cannot pay the rent with hundredfold zeros!

Remember the little widow in the Bible who came to the prophet and said, "My husband owed a debt, and he died, and now the creditors are coming to take my sons away because I owe this debt. What am I going to do?" (2 Kings 4:1-7)

The prophet asked, "What do you have?"

She said, "All that I have is a little bit of oil."

The prophet said, "That is enough."

God needed something to multiply.

Elisha said, "Send your boys to the neighbors to borrow every pot you possibly can. Then go into your house, shut the doors, and pour oil."

So they did as he said. They got all the pots they could find, went into the house, and closed the doors.

Then the widow took the little bit of oil she had and began to pour. She poured, and she poured, and she poured! She filled up every vessel she had. Finally, when she got to the last pot, the oil ran out. I believe that if she had enough pots to last until today, she would still be pouring oil! The oil did not run out until she ran out of vessels.

Then she went to the prophet and asked, "What do we do with all this oil!"

"Go sell it, pay your debts, and live on the rest."

She had an oil well in her kitchen, but she did not think she had anything at all that God could multiply.

There was another little widow whose neighbors were dying of hunger, because there was a famine in the land. She thought she might as well die of hunger, too. However, when she went out to get wood to build a fire for her last meal, she ran into a prophet of God. (1 Kings 17:10-24.)

The prophet said, "Make me a cake."

She said, "I cannot. I'm going to make cakes for my son and myself. We will eat and die, because this is all the oil and meal I have."

He said, "Make me a cake first."

If you will give God something first, He will multiply it. When she made the prophet a cake and gave it to him, she had enough left to make cakes for her son and herself. The prophet moved in with them and stayed there for about a year. Every breakfast, lunch, and dinner, they each had a cake. Nine cakes a day for 365 days made a total of 3,285 cakes — made out of almost nothing! God multiplied one cake into many cakes. He has to have something to multiply.

Two Sides to the Coin of Prosperity
• • •

Many people say, "I want to give, but I do not have anything to give."

What they really mean is that unless they change their standard of living, they do not have anything to give. But God will elevate your standard of living.

There are two sides to the coin of prosperity. There are many people teaching prosperity, but few tell you the other side of the coin says: "Responsibility." You are not to give to get rich or to have fun. You are to give in order to get rich to bless the world.

You plant, then you reap. You plant again and reap a bigger harvest. You plant a bigger field, so you can reap an even bigger harvest. In the meantime, while you are doing that, God is elevating your standard of living — and everybody around will know that God Almighty did it.

I get excited whenever I read Genesis, chapter 26. There was a famine in the land, and all the people were starving. They decided to go to Egypt to get something to eat; and Isaac, Abraham's son, decided that he would go to Egypt, too.

But God said, "Do not go there. Stay in the land I told your father that he could have, and I will honor the oath I made to Abraham."

Isaac was obedient. He remained there and planted in the land — and he reaped a hundredfold in the same year! He waxed great. He grew and became very great. He had great stores of herds and servants — and the Philistines envied him. This was because of God's covenant.

Have you ever had the Philistines envy you? You will, as soon as you start operating in the things of God and in His Word.

Your next-door neighbors and relatives will start saying, "I do not know how they do it. Coffee is high, gasoline is high, the cost of living is soaring, and there is sickness in the land. How do they do it?"

When the swine-flu bug first started, we were living in Mexico, and that is all you could hear: "The swine-flu is coming. It is the worst thing. It is terrible!"

While we were talking to a couple of ladies in West Texas, they asked, "Are you going to get your vaccination for swine-flu?"

I said, "I already got mine, a long time ago."

"How could you do that? It's a new vaccine."

I said, "The Bible says that no plague shall come nigh my dwelling. (Psalms 91:10.) I am vaccinated in the Word of God. I'm saturated with the blood of Jesus, and we do not allow sickness in our house."

Two Kinds of Giving
· · ·

There are two kinds of giving: giving of the known and giving of the unknown. There is obedient giving, and creative giving.

If God tells you to give $100 and you have it in your pocket, that does not take faith — it takes obedience. There is a blessing when you give of the known. Then, there is the time when God speaks to you and asks you to give $1,000.

You say, "Lord, I do not have $1,000, but I will give it. We will have to go into partnership. You supply it, and I will surely give it."

When you can do that, you have moved into a new dimension of giving. You will never know such a thrill until you do it. That is giving of the unknown — creative faith giving.

You will never be able to teach faith until you learn to live by faith. You will never learn to live by faith until you learn how to give by faith. I know from whence I came. Faith works by love.

Let me ask you three questions on saving a nest egg:

Who told you that you needed a nest egg? You did not find it in the Word of God. God's Word never says for you to provide for tomorrow. In fact, it always says the contrary. The Israelites asked for an ample supply of manna, but God only gave them a day's worth at a time.

If you have a nest egg, how large should it be — $10,000, $50,000, or what? One sickness could wipe it out. What tragedy are you believing for, and what will it cost?

How do you know your nest egg is not already rotten? You cannot put enough money in the bank to make anything off the interest. In the time it takes to draw interest, inflation has eaten it up.

There *is* one thing you can be absolutely certain of: If you plant a bigger field for the Gospel's sake, God will see to it that you reap a bigger harvest!

Are You a Conqueror or
More Than a Conqueror?
. . .

Christian, are you wearing more than the helmet of salvation?

I am excited about the armor of God. I feel sorry for people who know nothing about the Holy Spirit and are wearing the whole armor of God. Thank God for the helmet of salvation. But if you are standing out in a field with nothing on except the helmet of salvation, if you do not have on another spiritual stitch, the devil will run around taking pot shots at you with all of those fiery darts.

Just being saved will not help you win the battle. I believe we should win the battles down here. I believe in a positive God and a positive Gospel.

I believe in winning, and I believe we should win down here. I know it is going to be good when we get to heaven, but I want it to be good here on earth. I would be excited if God only told me I was a conqueror. But, Praise God, He said we are more than conquerors!

WHAT IS THE DIFFERENCE?
· · ·

When a prize fighter has an important fight coming up that is worth a lot of money to him, like a world championship, he will begin to train for that fight months in advance. When he trains, he will not look at, nor pay any attention to, anything else. He gives his whole life over to that one fight.

He will go off (apart) to training camp, away from everything. He watches what he eats; he does road work; he has sparring partners. Everything he does is geared to that one fight because, when the final bell rings, he wants to be the conqueror.

Everything he does is geared to the night when he will go into that ring and meet his opponent. He continues to train, and train, and train. Finally, the day comes. He goes into the arena and into the ring. The fighters are introduced, and the fight begins. He and his opponent fight and fight through many rounds.

Then the bell rings at last, and his hand is raised in victory. He is a conqueror! He may be cut. He may be bruised. He may be tired, but he is still the conqueror. He crawls out of the ring to the applause of all the people. He is still conqueror.

He walks back to the dressing room — still the conqueror. He takes a shower and puts on his clothes — still the conqueror. He walks over to the office to pick up the conqueror's check — all that money he got for winning!

Then, as the conqueror, he takes his check home. When he walks in the door, his wife comes over and kisses him, and he hands her the check. She is more than a conqueror!

He did all the work, went to all the trouble, fought the fight, and came out as a conqueror. The wife did not do anything, but she got all the money. She is more than a conqueror!

Do you see yourself and Jesus in there somewhere?

Jesus came and fought the fight. He whipped the devil hands down. He stripped Satan of every power he had, spoiled him, and made an open show of him. He spoiled principalities and powers and took every bit of power away from the devil and his demons. (Colossians 2:15, Matthew 28:18.)

Then what do you think Jesus did with all that power? He did not take it back to heaven with Him. He gave it to the Church! He gave it to you and me.

He said, "I came out of this thing as Conqueror. I have whipped the devil. I defeated him. I took the keys to death, hell, and the grave. I stripped the devil of all his power. He cannot do anything more. It is all mine; I am Conqueror."

Then He said to us, "You did not do anything, but you are more than a conqueror. You take My name. You take this power. You go, heal the sick, and raise the dead. You preach the Gospel around the world. You are more than conquerors."

JESUS DID IT FOR US
· · ·

Many people talk about faith preachers being arrogant, cocky, and prideful. But when I think of the unlimited power of the God of the universe dwelling inside me, it makes me straighten my shoulders and walk tall.

There is no way in the world that you could get me to cross the Rio Grande River into Mexico (or any other country) without God. You could not get me to cross the border — not even to buy a souvenir — without God.

But I have the unlimited God of the universe dwelling on the inside of me. I have the Word of God that says, "Go and preach the Gospel." So I can cross that border — walking, driving, or flying — and it does not bother me a bit.

I just say, "Look out, devil, here I come."

That is the attitude every Christian should have. We should not be running from the devil; he should be running from us!

God gave me a vision once of one of those old ships in which the Spanish conquerors sailed when they set out to discover a new land. They would anchor the ship offshore, get into a rowboat, and row to the land.

Then they would take their flag, stick it into the ground, and say, "I claim this in the name of the king."

God told me to do that.

He said, "When you go into an area or some country, take the Christian flag, walk in there, plant it deep into the ground, and say, 'I claim this for King Jesus!' and run the devil off."

That is the way we operate our ministry. Every time we go into a place, especially if I am flying in a private plane, I will circle the place several times and say, "We bring down the prince of the power of the air, because we are taking over this place while we are here." God always confirms His Word.

Take these principles I have shared with you. Use them to help yourself and others — and remember: If you are a Christian, you have the unlimited God of the universe living inside you. That makes you not a loser, but *more than a conqueror!*

Dr. Terry L. Mize

Pure religion and undefiled before God and the Father is this, to visit the fatherless and widows in their affliction, and to keep himself unspotted from the world. James 1:27

Open thy mouth for the dumb in the cause of all such as are appointed to destruction. Open thy mouth, judge righteously, and plead the cause of the poor and needy. Proverbs 31:8-9

These three verses of scripture are the essence of what makes Dr. Terry L. Mize tick; the reasons he does all that he does for the King and His Kingdom.

Nearly 50 years ago, Terry began his ministry in the jungles of Panama, bringing the Gospel to a primitive tribe. In 1969, he and his bride Jackie were married and spent several years in Mexico before God began to reveal to them that to reach the world, as He had commanded, they had to move back to the U.S. and begin to travel to many nations.

Now, Terry Mize Ministries has preached the Gospel on six continents and is heavily involved all over the world in places such as Romania, Ukraine, India, Zimbabwe, Thailand, Cuba, Haiti, Jamaica, and always Terry's "first love," Mexico.

Terry and Jackie are both best-selling authors. Terry wrote "More Than Conquerors," which includes the much-told "Hitchhiker Story," and Jackie's legacy can be witnessed through the countless testimonies from her book, "Supernatural Childbirth."

Out of Terry and Jackie's love for the orphans they encounter in their travels, they established the Jackie Mize International Children's Foundation in 2000, through which they support children's homes in India and Romania, and provide humanitarian relief where it is urgently needed. (www.jmicf.org)

Brother Terry has served on many missions and ministry boards and is a founding father of both the International Convention of Faith Ministries and Victory World Missions Training Center. Miracles and healings have followed Terry throughout his apostolic ministry as he goes about giving Living Bread to dying men around the world, teaching the integrity of God's Word without compromise.

In 2013, Terry's beloved wife Jackie passed away and he has since remarried. Renee Garner Mize is a powerful woman of the Word, a prolific Bible teacher and a blessing to the Mize family. With nearly 50 years of experience in ministry of her own, she and her late husband Dean have been close friends of the family for decades. As Dean and Jackie both went to Heaven, it seemed only natural that Terry and Renee would join forces. They have hit the ground running and are joyfully doing God's work together.

Terry and Renee live in Tulsa, OK and have 7 children and 14 grandchildren between them.

To contact Terry Mize
for a catalog of teaching materials
or to order additional copies of
More Than Conquerors,
write to:

Terry Mize Ministries
P.O. Box 35044
Tulsa, OK 74153

Phone: (918) 392-9930

Email: mizeterry@aol.com
www.terrymizeministries.org

For more information about the
Jackie Mize International Children's Foundation,
write to:

JMICF
P.O. Box 35044
Tulsa, OK 74153

Phone: Toll-free (855) 76-JMICF (56423)

Email: info@jmicf.org
www.jmicf.org

Please include your prayer requests
and testimonies when you write.